'This is a beautiful story – it radiates with inspiration and proves that much good can still be done on earth.'

President Vaclav Havel

'I am very pleased with the excellent book *Nicholas Winton and the Rescued Generation*. It is not only a profound biography of Mr Winton showing him in all his complexities, his origins, the story of his rescue operation and his post-war career, but it also depicts the touching stories of the rescued children and his collaborators. It is a masterful account of an ordinary man who did extraordinary things.'

Matej Mináč
December 2002

'One story has the power to move me to tears, no matter how often I hear it, or retell it. It is the story of Sir Nicholas Winton, and the 699 children he saved from the Nazi Holocaust … It is a unique story, and a wonderful book. Above all, its hero is a man who has inspired millions of people to believe that one man can make a difference, if he has energy, vision and compassion.'

Esther Rantzen
January 2003

 **Muriel Emanuel**, born in London, worked as an editor of art reference books before becoming a freelance writer and researcher. Her publications include: *Israel: A Survey and Bibliography*, 1971, and *Contemporary Architects*, 1980 and 1994.

 **Vera Gissing** was born in Prague in 1928. She escaped to Britain in 1939 on one of the eight Winton trains. An author of children's books and a literary translator, she is widely known for her autobiography *Pearls of Childhood*, published in 1988 and now in its eleventh edition, and for her work in Holocaust education.

Nicholas Winton and the Rescued Generation

'SAVE ONE LIFE, SAVE THE WORLD'

(adapted from the Talmud)

'WHOEVER SAVED ONE IS AS THOUGH
HE SAVED A UNIVERSE'

(Mishna Sanhedrin 37a)

Nicholas Winton
and the
Rescued Generation

The Story of 'Britain's Schindler'

MURIEL EMANUEL
and
VERA GISSING

Foreword
ESTHER RANTZEN

VALLENTINE MITCHELL
LONDON • PORTLAND, OR

First published in 2002 in Great Britain by
VALLENTINE MITCHELL
Crown House, 47 Chase Side
Southgate, London N14 5BP

and in the United States of America by
VALLENTINE MITCHELL
c/o ISBS, 5824 N.E. Hassalo Street
Portland, Oregon 97213-3644

Website: www.vmbooks.com

Reprinted 2002, 2003

British Library Cataloguing in Publication Data

Emanuel, Muriel
    Nicholas Winton and the rescued generation: the story of
    'Britain's Schindler'
    1. Winton, Nicholas 2. Righteous Gentiles in the Holocaust
    3. Jewish children in the Holocaust 4. Jewish children
    Czech Republic 5. Bankers – Great Britain – Biography
    6. Philanthropists – Great Britain – Biography
    I. Title II. Gissing, Vera, 1928–
    940.5'318'092

ISBN 0-85303-438-9 (cloth)
ISBN 0-85303-425-7 (paper)

Library of Congress Cataloging-in-Publication Data:

Emanuel, Muriel
    Nicholas Winton and the rescued generation: the story of
    'Britain's Schindler' / Muriel Emanuel and Vera Gissing.
        p. cm.
    ISBN 0-85303-425-7 (pbk.)
    1. Winton, Nicholas, 1909– 2. Jews – England – Biography. 3. World War,
    1939–1945 – Jews – Rescue – Great Britain. 4. Refugees, Jewish – Great
    Britain. 5. Kindertransports (Rescue operations). 6. Holocaust, Jewish
    (1939–1945) – Czechoslovakia.
    I. Gissing, Vera. II. Title

DS135.E6 W564 2001
940.53'18'092 – dc 21
[B]   2001051218

Typeset in 11/13pt ZapfCalligraphica by Frank Cass Publishers
Printed and bound in Great Britain by
MPG Books Ltd, Bodmin, Cornwall

Contents

PART ONE
by Muriel Emanuel

Contents

Illustrations

Between pages 52 and 53:

1. Nicholaus Wertheim, Winton's paternal grandfather.
2. Rudolf Wertheim, Winton's father, c.1900.
3. In the garden at Cleve Road; Winton with his maternal grandmother, Aunt Ida, Uncle Emil, and sister, Lottie, c.1910.
4. Rudolf Wertheim in British Army uniform, c.1916.
5. Watch innards and other items of no value being thrown overboard. Winton is on the right, wearing glasses.
6. Watch innards, having been removed from their gold or silver cases.
7. Winton and his mother, Barbara, 1948.
8. Winton fencing, c.1931. This was his favourite sport, in which he excelled.
9. Winton's mother working in the London office, c.1939.
10. Winton and co-drivers during his time with the ambulance service in France, 1940.
11. Winton with his brother and sister in Willow Road, Hampstead, c.1942.
12. Grete and Nicky Winton on their wedding day, October 1948.
13. Grete, Nicky, Nicky's sister and brother and Grete's sister, Kirsten, 1948.
14. The famous scrapbook, discovered in Winton's attic in 1988, detailing events in 1938–39.
15. February 1939 report on the problem of refugee children in Czechoslovakia, signed by Winton.
16. Circular letter, June 1939. This was sent to other committees for refugees.
17. Examples of other committees in operation at the time.

Between pages 148 and 149:

18. Contents page of document containing particulars of 400 urgent cases, produced by the British Committee for Refugees from Czechoslovakia, Children's Section.
19. Young person's document of identity, issued by the United Kingdom (both sides shown).

Vera outside Vera Gissing's cottage during the filming of *Into the Arms of Strangers*, in which Winton and Vera's sister both feature. Nicholas' role in the film was relatively small, but he was the only rescuer to feature in it. (Courtesy of Sabine Films Incorporated. Photo by Cayce Callaway.)

33. The premiere of *Into the Arms of Strangers*, London, November 2000. Nicholas Winton with Prince Charles.

34. Nicholas Winton with Dr Elizabeth Maxwell and Matej Minác at the ICA premiere of *All My Loved Ones*, London, 1999.

10 DOWNING STREET
LONDON SW1A 2AA

THE PRIME MINISTER

5 September 2002

Dear Mr. Winton,

I am delighted that the documentary film about you is being shown publicly for the first time in Britain. This film is long-overdue recognition of your extraordinary humanitarian achievement in saving hundreds of Czechoslovak children from death.

Your initiative and determination in the months leading to the outbreak of the Second World War remain an inspiration. The selfless commitment you showed, and steadfast will to ask "What can I do to help?", and then to act, are examples to us all. That you did it in the face of seemingly insurmountable odds makes what you did all the more remarkable.

The people you saved, and their children, many thousands together, are a living and heartwarming testament to your courage.

Thank you for all you have done.

Yours sincerely,

Tony Blair

Mr Nicholas Winton

Nicholas Winton being presented with the Tomas Garrigue Masaryk Order, the most prestigious award in the Czech Republic, by President Vaclav Havel, October 1998.

Tribute by Vaclav Havel
President of the Czech Republic

On the morning of 28 October 1998, Nicholas Winton was granted a private audience with President Vaclav Havel in his office at Hradcany Castle. Spontaneously, this is what the President said (the words, spoken in Czech, have been translated into English):

'This is a beautiful story – it radiates with inspiration and proves that much good can still be done on this earth. I have the impression that it is quite exceptional when in an ordinary businessman such feelings of humanity are suddenly awakened – also great wisdom and foresight – and he impulsively undertakes and accomplishes such a deed as you, Mr Winton, have done, because you became aware of the danger which threatened the children. The majority would not have survived the Holocaust. You organised and subsequently put into operation their transports to the West; it is remarkable that you spontaneously understood how essential it was to do this.'

Acknowledgements

I am grateful to the helpful staff at the Wiener Library in London when researching the Wertheim and Wertheimer families from Germany.

I have interviewed many people whilst preparing the manuscript and hope I will be forgiven if I do not mention them all individually.

I had a meeting with Dr Johanna Collis in County Wicklow, who helped enormously with her memories of Barbara, Nicky's mother; telephone conversations with Helen Dickermann in Levit Town, New York sorted out various problem areas relating to Nicky's time with the International Refugee Organisation; near and distant relatives gave me their time, particularly Nicky's brother, Robert, who laid the ground for the family tree, without whom I would not have been able to have so clear a picture of the wider family connection.

I owe a debt to Professor John Röhl, of Sussex University, who supplied further details of Dr Ida McAlpine (Nicky's aunt).

Vera and I have had Nicky's co-operation throughout. Despite his 92 years, he continues to impress us with his sharp mind and his memory for detail; a constant 'jotter' of notes at important and not so important times of his life, he has provided us with aspects of events that otherwise we may have been denied.

Muriel Emanuel
August 2001

Acknowledgements

My deepest gratitude to Nicky Winton – for saving my life and for becoming a vital, cherished part of it! After we met in 1988, I felt compelled to research and spread the story of his incredible deed; thus I gladly joined Muriel in writing this book which we hope will be a fitting tribute to the compassionate man who throughout his life showed the world the true meaning of humanity …

My thanks to the 'Winton children' for their co-operation, and to Charles Chadwick for his help.

Vera Gissing

FAMILY TREE

David Alexander FIORINO = Hanna Marburg
b.1770 Göttingen d.1848 Cassel | 1775–1821

Leon WERTHEIM = Glückhilde FIORINO
b.19.10.1785 Eschwege | b.1803 Kassel
d.17.7.1848 Hanau | d.1883 Kassel

Abraham David
1805–84

Jeremias David
Alexander
(miniaturist)
1797–1847

Salomon
David
1798–1827

Joel
1800–41

Nicholaus = Charlotte KAHN
b.20.1.1836 Hanau | b. 17.4.1846
d.1919 London | Eschwege

Sigmund WERTHEIMER = Mathilda LUST
b.5.11.1850 | b.30.11.1861
d.24.6.23 Nürnberg | d.1940 UK

Friedel (Wertham)
= Florence Hesketh

Emil
= Katie

Ida* 1899–1974
= 1. Hirschmann
2. Hendl
3. McAlpine

Paul 1900–40
= 'Toos'

Hannah

Sacha

Bruno (Wertham = Muriel)

Rudolf (Rudi) = Barbara (Babi) WERTHEIMER
b.19/26.7.1881 Moscow | b. 4.4.1888 Nurenberg
d.1936 London | d. 1979 London

married c. 1907

Charlotte Matilda
(Lottie)
b.1908 London
d.14.2.1996 London

Nicholas (Nicky)
b.19.5.09 London
(*The family changed its
name to Winton
in 1938*)
=Grete Gjelstrup
b.1919 Denmark
d.27.8.99 Maidenhead

Robert (Bobby)
b. 23.10.1914 London
=Heather Charlton
b. 1920 India

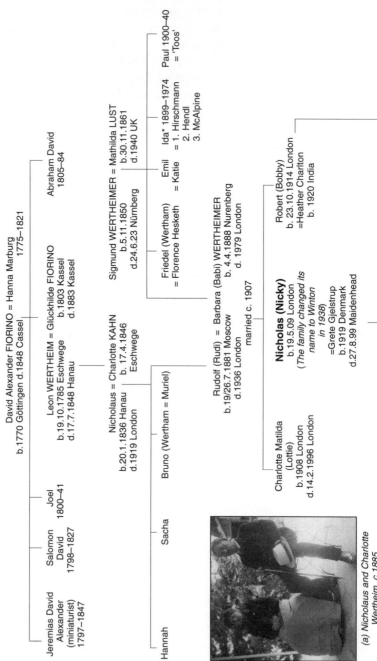

(a) Nicholaus and Charlotte
Wertheim, c.1885

Nicholas (Nick) b. 1952
= Caroline Adair (div.)

Barbara b. 1953
= Stephen Watson

Robin 1956-62

Laurence   Holly

Peter b. 1954
=Christine Barnes

Andrew b.1956

Carol b.1958

Laura
b.1978

Adam
b.1979

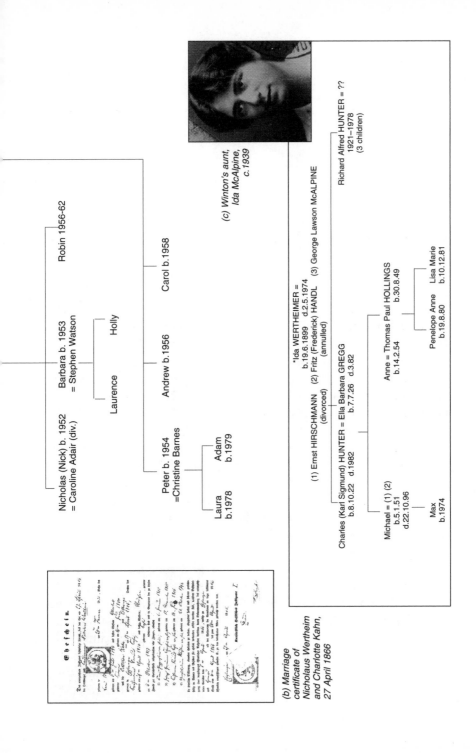

(c) Winton's aunt,
Ida McAlpine,
c.1939

*Ida WERTHEIMER =
b.19.6.1899 d.2.5.1974

(1) Ernst HIRSCHMANN   (2) Fritz (Frederick) HANDL   (3) George Lawson McALPINE
(divorced)   (annulled)

Charles (Karl Sigmund) HUNTER = Ella Barbara GREGG
b.8.10.22 d.1982   b.7.7.26 d.3.82

Richard Alfred HUNTER = ??
1921–1978
(3 children)

Michael = (1) (2)
b.5.1.51
d.22.10.96

Anne = Thomas Paul HOLLINGS
b.14.2.54   b.30.8.49

Max
b.1974

Penelope Anne
b.19.8.80

Lisa Marie
b.10.12.81

(b) Marriage
certificate of
Nicholaus Wertheim
and Charlotte Kahn,
27 April 1866

Publisher's Note

The third revised edition of *Nicholas Winton and the Rescued Generation* has been published for several reasons (in addition, of course, to meeting the international demand from readers following the wide publicity surrounding the Nicholas Winton story). Firstly, to coincide with the award of a knighthood to Nicholas Winton in the 2003 New Year Honours List, a much-merited honour. Secondly, to mark the new television film by Esther Rantzen for Carlton Television, *Winton's Children*, which will be shown as part of the official British Holocaust Memorial Day, 27 January 2003. (Esther Rantzen had first revealed the great humanitarian work carried out by Nicholas Winton 50 years earlier in her programme, *That's Life*, aired in 1988.) Thirdly, to celebrate the award of an 'Emmy' for best documentary in New York in November 2002 to the outstanding and award winning Czech film producer Matej Mináč for *Nicholas Winton: The Power of Good*. His devoted and pioneering films have helped bring the work of Nicholas Winton to public notice, and has also brought much credit and honour to the Czech film making profession. My thanks go to all those who provided, and gave permission for the publishing of, several personal photographs reproduced in the book; and I am grateful for the speed with which everyone who contributed to this third edition – Muriel Emanuel, Vera Gissing, Esther Rantzen, Matej Mináč and Sir Nicholas Winton – provided their new and updated material in order to meet a most demanding deadline. My thanks to the 'professionals all'.

Frank Cass
January 2003

Foreword

Esther Rantzen and Nicholas Winton during the filming of Winton's Children, *2002, which is to be aired as part of the official British Holocaust Memorial Day, 2003. (Courtesy of Mark Bourdillion/Carlton Television.)*

One story has the power to move me to tears, no matter how often I hear it, or retell it. It is the story of Sir Nicholas Winton, and the 669 children he saved from the Nazi Holocaust. I first heard it in 1988, when Nicholas had just rediscovered an album in his loft, and leafed through its pages to find precious photographs and documents belonging to those children. The children were now, 50 years after their dramatic rescue, scattered all over the world. Nicholas believed that his album might contain their only records of their families and their childhood, and that we might be able to contact them via the programme I was making at that time, *That's Life!*. So he contacted me, and my production team set to work to try and track them down. We invited Nicholas himself to our studio, without revealing to him our plan, that we would sit him in the front row, surrounded by the children he had saved and introduce them to him for the first time on the programme. Nicholas is famously modest and unassuming. I believe he has still not forgiven me.

I am unrepentant. The moment when Vera Gissing turned to him, kissed him and thanked him for her life was unforgettable. Until that moment, she and other children he saved had no idea that it was Nicholas who organized the trains that carried them to safety, persuaded the British Home Secretary to allow them to enter Britain, found the families who fostered them, forged the permits that got them over the border out of Czechoslovakia, and still mourns the 250 children on the last, ninth train which was turned back at the border on the day war was declared. For the first time 'Winton's Children' knew how and why they had been rescued, and realized that there were hundreds of others who also escaped a terrible death in the Nazi camps. That moment in our television studio has inspired me and has held a very special place in my memory ever since. It encapsulates the truth that makes life worth living, that no matter how bleak the news and hard the times, goodness and courage can emerge even from the depth and darkness of the holocaust. That message, that hope, is embodied in the story of Nicholas Winton.

As I write, Nicholas has just, at long last, received the recognition he deserves as a national hero, and a national treasure. He has been knighted in the New Year's Honour's list, at the age of 93, and he is the subject of an hour-long television documentary, *Winton's Children*, celebrating his achievements, the making of which has been, for me, a labour of love. It is not easy to pay tribute to this man, who rejects praise because he claims he did nothing special and is embarrassed by the spotlight because he

Foreword

is essentially a private man. But during the making of the documentary, as I met the survivors he rescued and retraced their journey from Prague, I discovered that Winton's children provide the living evidence of his achievement. Vera Gissing is among the most eloquent. I will never forget her description of her arrival as a child in Liverpool Street Station, to be greeted there by a little woman she had never met before, who told her, in a language she did not yet understand, 'You will be loved.' And she was.

Vera has described her own life and the lives of many other rescued children with great power and vividness, and in this book you can read the extraordinary story she has written in collaboration with Muriel Emanuel, of the young stockbroker who went for a holiday to Prague, and ended up saving a generation of Czech-Jewish children.

It is a unique story, and a wonderful book. Above all, its hero is a man who has inspired millions of people to believe that one man can make a difference, if he has energy, vision and compassion. Edmund Burke said, 'For the triumph of evil, it is only necessary that good men do nothing.' Sir Nicholas Winton is a good man who acted when others allowed evil to triumph, and through his action, provides an example for humanity.

Esther Rantzen
January 2003

Preface

My fascination with the life of Nicholas Winton – and the inspiration behind my film, *Nicholas Winton: The Power of Good* – sprang from the book *Pearls of Childhood* by Vera Gissing, which totally changed my life. This is a powerful and touching account of the unusual life of a little girl whose wonderful childhood was destroyed by the worst events of the previous century and who was miraculously saved by one man – Nicholas Winton.

When I read about him, I was immediately convinced that this was a great story. I wanted to know what films had been made about this unique rescue operation. I got in touch with Doris Koziskova and she told me that the best way to get a direct answer to this question would be to contact Vera Gissing. Getting in touch with Vera was the beginning of our long friendship and collaboration. Vera told me that no film had ever made about Nicholas Winton. This information astounded me. But, Vera said, that she was working on a book about this man and she had researched extensively in the archives and conducted many interviews with Winton. As a filmmaker I immediately felt an urge to put Mr Winton's story onto film. Vera enthusiastically promised to cooperate and to show me all her material. Seeing her work on the Winton rescue mission really astonished me. She also took me to meet Winton personally. I expected to meet a 'hero', but instead I had found somebody much more surprising – an ordinary man with a great sense of humour. You could talk with him on many subjects – from gardening, films, or opera to sports. I remember that I spent most of the time laughing at his jokes. Vera has been very devoted to this man who rescued her sister and herself. Although she only became personally acquainted with him in 1988 her life was totally transformed by learning about him. She started to lecture on him at schools. She wanted very much to pay tribute to this unique man; and wanted to thank him by writing a book on him. It had become a sort of a mission for her. *Nicholas Winton and the Rescued Generation*, which Vera wrote with Muriel Emanuel, was published in 2002. I must tell you: I, and my collaborators, Martina Stolbova and Patrik Pass, were drawn in by her enthusiasm.

Because Vera was willing to give us a hand and even to write the first draft of a script for a documentary on Winton, we decided to make a film on him. Finally, we made two films. The first one was a feature film, *All My Loved Ones* (produced by Jiri Bartoska and Rudolf Biermann, the role of Winton being played by Rupert Graves), which depicts a fictional story of one Czech child who was rescued by Winton. One of the most moving moments in the film is the scene in which the little hero packs for a trip to Britain. His mother brings him a precious present – an empty diary – explaining that, through this diary, they could communicate even in the moments they were separated. I took this scene, with the permission of Vera, from her autobiographical book. The film was a Slovak nominee for the Oscar competition and was awarded 14 prestigious prizes presented during more than 65 film festivals. This film is currently on show in the USA. The second film was a documentary picture: *Nicholas Winton: The Power of Good*. Thanks to Vera we had unique material and access to the rescued children all over the world. She encouraged us during the three years we needed to complete the film. We had the good fortune to have one of the rescued children, Joe Schlesinger, as the narrator and guide to the film. My crew, Vera and Joe had a very challenging task: to make a film that would faithfully reconstruct the Prague rescue mission and show how one man's courage and determination could 'change the history'. It was not only thrilling work for all of us; we also felt we had a certain duty to do our best to finish the documentary and, in this way, to thank Mr Winton for his extraordinary efforts to save Czech children before the outbreak of World War II. I hope that we have managed to achieve this aim.

The world première of *The Power of Good* took place at the International Palm Springs Film Festival in January 2002 as the official closing film of the festival. It was also shown in Los Angeles at the Wiesenthal Center (where Mr Winton was presented the Wiesenthal Prize), and in New York at the Symphony Place in a 900-seat theatre. Ten ambassadors from the countries in which the rescued children now live took part. Mr Winton was awarded the Certificate of Merit by the Governor of New York, George Pataki, and had a private audience with Hilary and Bill Clinton.

The Czechoslovakian première took place in Laterna Magika and the film was also screened at the Karlove Vary International Film Festival. The film was then presented at the Barbican Film Season in London, where Mr Winton was presented with a framed letter of thanks written by Prime Minister Tony Blair. The film was voted the twelfth most popular film, from 300 mostly feature films, by audiences at the Vancouver Film Festival and won the Audience Award at the Washington Jewish Film Festival in 2002. On 25 November in New York we were presented with the International Emmy Award for the best documentary of 2002. We feel that this prestigious prize belongs in the first place to Nicholas Winton, to a brave man, who – at a time when great darkness was descending upon Europe – stood up against evil. It was an honour for all of us to have the privilege of working on such an extraordinary story and I wish personally to thank Vera for her incredible support without which neither of the films would have been made.

I am very pleased with the excellent book *Nicholas Winton and the Rescued Generation*. It is not only a profound biography of Mr Winton showing him in all his complexities, his origins, the story of his rescue operation and his post-war career, but it also depicts the touching stories of the rescued children and his collaborators. It is a masterful account of an ordinary man who did extraordinary things.

Matej Mináč
December 2002

Matej Mináč (on the right) being presented with the Emmy for best documentary of 2002 for Nicholas Winton: The Power of Good, *25 November, at the International Emmy Awards Gala, Sheraton Hotel, New York.*

Note

I am delighted that the years of work put in by Muriel Emanuel and Vera Gissing are being rewarded by a third edition of their thoughtful book. Also, as the story gets wider known, so many more of the *kinder* get in touch and some can be reunited with their friends from bygone days. For me, it is always a thrill to hear from them and I can only hope they understand and excuse me for not writing to them.

Sir Nicholas Winton
December 2002

Introduction to the First Edition

What kind of man, on two weeks leave from a secure job, with a contented and comfortable life, involves himself in a situation that most of us, however strong our compassion, would walk away from, believing that on our own we could do nothing?

Nicholas Winton has been called 'Britain's Schindler', but *he* had no power, no riches, no factory where he could employ threatened Jews, nor did he have access to exit permits as did the Swede Raoul Wallenburg in Hungary and the Japanese Chiune Sugihara in Lithuania, who were both diplomats. The very essence of this man's deed lay in the fact that here was this young stockbroker on holiday who, when faced with a desperate situation, was torn apart and decided there *was* something he could do – or at least try.

'Off the M40 at Exit 4, follow the signs to Marlow, then to Maidenhead.' These were my instructions. It was late February 1996 and the trees were still in winter mood, their interwoven tracery breaking the skyline. The snow of the previous weeks could still be seen and primroses were cheekily popping their heads through the slush; sturdy spikes of daffodil leaves gave hope for the spring that still seemed far ahead; the car heater arrow was full on red. I was on my way to meet Nicholas Winton.

'Pass two pubs, Golden Ball on the right, Robin Hood on the left', what could be more English? I drove through a gate of what had been a grand estate, now divided into various plots; roses, clematis and wisteria were neatly pinned to the walls of the modest houses built on this acreage – hardly distinguishable in their winter nakedness. The original eighteenth-century rough-hewn walls surround the garden of Winton's house built 30 years earlier and behind it, an ancient mulberry tree threw its bare branches haphazardly in all directions; I was later to taste its exuberant fruits. All lay dormant awaiting the spring sunshine. All very English.

I had only recently read about Winton; his tale of the rescue of a great number of children living in Czechoslovakia in 1939 whose lives were in peril; how he had given little thought to this 'job' during the following 50 years and how his wife, whilst clearing out the loft, had come across myriad papers, not only relating to the *kindertransport*, but to many other extraordinary and interesting facets of his life. He was reluctant to dispose of them; his children were not able to undertake the task of sorting them through and he wanted someone to help put them in order.

I was intrigued – I wanted to meet this man.

* * *

Winton was 86 when I first met him; fine looking, stocky, but upright, grey haired, bespectacled, kindly and with a most gentle nature. His manners and appearance, that of an Englishman born and bred with a long family pedigree; public-school educated, possibly followed by a career in the civil service or banking; in retirement, a doyen of the church and local and national charities? I was reminded of one of Mrs Dalloway's guests: 'No country but England could have produced him – a perfect specimen of the public school type.' Maybe Virginia Woolf would not have been fooled. My first impressions were not to be entirely upheld.

English born he was, in Hampstead, where he spent his childhood and attended preparatory school. Educated at Stowe, he did briefly pursue a career in banking. Numerous articles have been written about him; he has been referred to as 'the reserved Englishman' and 'the epitome of an Englishman'. But despite all these hints, I was to discover otherwise. Winton's German-Jewish paternal grandparents had settled in the United

Kingdom in the 1860s. His mother arrived in this country from Nürnberg in 1907. Until I came on the scene in 1996, little mention had been made of his family background.

Winton had retired early and made his life in this rural setting, commuting distance from London, shared with his devoted wife, Grete, to whom he had been married for almost 50 years. He lived a relaxed, but active life, tending the abundantly planted garden and at the time of our meeting was still growing his own vegetables.

He has found life hard since Grete died in 1999, but continues with his activities and enjoys the visits of his children and grandchildren. He also enjoys the visits of his other 'children', now in their late sixties and seventies who owe their lives to him; some of the 669 brought to these shores from a troubled Prague in 1939 by a dedicated and committed young man of 29, months, weeks and later only days prior to the declaration of World War II.

My first inkling of Winton's existence took place early in 1996 when I was handed a letter he had written to a journalist who was preparing an article about him for her paper. He had asked her if she knew anyone who could help him sort his papers. I had just completed editing a mammoth tome and was reluctant to take on anything as pressurised for the moment. This looked as if it could be something I could do at leisure and fill in a few months before getting back to a book I had been playing about with for some time.

At our meeting, however, it was obvious that Winton had a book in mind and whilst I felt confident to tackle the biography of this unassuming man, I was convinced that I was not the person to take on the story of the *kindertransports*. I did, however, know exactly who would be capable of undertaking this task.

I had read Vera Gissing's very moving testimony *Pearls of Childhood*, based on diaries she had kept throughout the war, but had not yet met her. I did know that since Winton re-entered her life in 1988 she had become increasingly involved in his life and work. She was enthusiastic about the project and the proposal for us to work together on the book has proved to be, without doubt, the best decision I could have made. It has taken us four years to put the story together as both of us have been busy with other commitments. We have been determined to get the facts right and this has required considerable research. So many misleading reports have appeared in the press since the story of the Winton *kindertransports* came to light in 1988. Articles concentrating on the saving of the children have appeared in newspapers and journals; there have been broadcasts and interviews on television both in London and Prague. A feature film incorporating Winton's efforts, made in Prague, was premiered there in 1999. Time and time again the question has been asked 'Why don't we know more about this man?'

I set out to discover his family background and became so absorbed with his antecedents that I found myself digressing. Initially, this information did not seem to have any relevance to the story about to be told, but I came to realise that many of these facts did play an important part in the shaping of Winton's life and his character. In my researches at the Weiner Library in London, I came upon material of which Winton himself was unaware. He remarked, in his modest way 'You are finding my family more interesting than me!'

At first, I had thought of this book as a straightforward biography, but soon realised that the story of the *kindertransports* should dominate the narrative and not just appear chronologically as if it was yet another event in Winton's long life. Even the smallest details of the rescue mission are certain to be of interest. My task was his life story, Vera's those eight months from December 1938 to September 1939 and the period following the scenes shown on Esther Rantzen's programme *That's Life!* in 1988 portraying Winton's first meeting with some of the children who owed their lives to him.

The chapter 'The Re-Awakening' was not in our original plans – it simply evolved but we see it as a very important part of the tale. After all, lives were saved, but what happened to those lives and the difficulties that had to be faced are as meaningful and significant as the problems and intricacies presented to the team who effected the rescue mission.

There is an an abrupt change in style and temperament from Winton's background, early years and youth to the rescue mission covering those packed months in 1939 followed by the stories of some of the children he saved. We hope that the reader will sympathise with our problem and appreciate the relevance of the background details of Winton's life to his great deed which resulted in him saving what could be considered a generation of Czech Jews.

Winton is a very private person, of immense warmth and compassion, but reticent and reluctant to talk about his emotions experienced either at the time of the events we are discussing or at the present moment. Over the years we have built up a relationship of trust, each of us giving and taking in as equal parts as has been possible. By the very nature of my work preparing this manuscript it has been necessary to dig and delve into a life, though full to the brim of interest and, at times excitement, considered to be one of comparative ordinariness by the very person about whom I was writing. I have found it immensely difficult not to feel an intruder.

I was some months into the project when Winton announced that he did have some diaries. 'I don't think you will find them of much interest – just schoolboy's jottings' he said. Yes, they were schoolboy's jottings, but diaries such as these and his notes from a later period were stuff that bring joy to any biographer. However, in order to make our story of interest to a wider public, I have, not happily, had to invade areas that he would have preferred to be left hidden. Grete gave me enormous encouragement and help in this direction.

There are many tales to tell about this extraordinary man whose life was turned around by a chance visit to a foreign country at a pitiable time in its history. His experiences have been varied and not without excitement and risk, but the humanitarian element has been constant throughout.

Winton has received many awards, most of them unrelated to the 1939 rescue mission. In 1983, five years before the Prague story came to light, he was awarded an MBE for services to the community; in 1999, he received the Freedom of the City of Windsor, an honour he shares almost exclusively with the Queen, the Duke of Edinburgh, Prince Charles and the Queen Mother. It was to take five decades before the greatest of his humanitarian deeds was to be recognised. In 1991 he received the Freedom of the City of Prague and seven years later the Tomas Garrigue Masaryk Award, the most prestigious award in the Czech Republic, presented by President Havel in a grand ceremony at the Hradcany Castle in Prague. A more expected title, the Israeli honour of Righteous Gentile, however, eludes him. First, it is necessary to be a gentile; second, the saving of lives must have taken place within an occupied country when your own life would have been endangered. It is curious and, in the first instance, complex, to think that this brave, committed man does not fulfil either of those criteria.

Muriel Emanuel
May 2001

Introduction (I) to the Third Edition

In the Spring of 2001, five years after my first meeting with Nicky Winton and my initial resolve to tell the story of his life, I handed in the manuscript to the publishers. I was anxious to return to some work that had been interrupted and put the Winton story behind me. But it was not to work that way. The stories of the children on the Winton transports had consumed me and I was, to a degree, traumatised. I could see the scars that have become the legacy of these 'children' and their children and even the children of the third generation. Maybe I could have eased *my* way out and move on, but *they* have no way out.

The timing of the publication has been fortuitous. Two films by Matej Mináč, particularly the documentary *The Power of Good*, and the numerous events that have taken place in the past year have generated interest and curiosity in Winton and his mission. Since the initial launch at the London Jewish Cultural Centre, there have been events at various venues including the Embassy of the Czech Republic, University of Sussex, Imperial War Museum and the Barbican Centre, where Peter Hain, then Minister of State for Europe, presented Nicky with a letter of recognition from the Prime Minister.

At 93, Nicky takes all this in his stride; his energy and enthusiasm are phenomenal. Ever ready for a new adventure, he flew Concorde to New York for the showing of the film *The Power of Good* in September 2002. Whilst there, he attended a reception for Vaclav Havel, President of the Czech Republic, at which Bill and Hilary Clinton were present. Nicky, whom Hilary had expressed a wish to meet, was ushered into a small room and

xxxv

presented to the Clintons where they chatted comfortably about many things, including the Barak/Arafat meeting and the unfortunate events in Israel.

We are good friends – Nicky and I – both passionate about music (particularly Wagner) and keen gardeners, but there are some areas that continue to cause me bewilderment. The hero I chose to study and write about has been an elusive subject; there was a point at which we almost decided to abandon the project. He had problems relating to almost anything that he had not given thought to for so long or maybe ever. Today I do believe he has come to terms with his background and it now gives him enormous pleasure to see his own children and grandchildren sharing his new experiences and the publicity that has come his way. I had almost no contact with Nick and Barbara whilst researching for the book; they knew so little of their father's greatest deed and were confused by the details that were emerging about their family background. As I have said before, in the original introduction, I felt an intruder.

In recent months both Nicky's son and daughter have participated in the events that have taken place. It was only when the papers were found in 1988 that, along with their mother, they became fully aware of Winton's venture in Czechoslovakia before World War II. 'It was then', says Nick, 'that I realised the full implication of his work in saving so many lives. It has been a delight to be with him in his new role as a father figure to so many of his *kinder* and to support him in attending the many functions to which he is invited.'

Barbara practices as a homeopath in Herefordshire where she lives with her husband and two children. Although further away from the hub of activity that has surrounded her father in the last 14 years she has found that, 'The book has been a talking point with friends and colleagues and has provoked their interest in their own family stories from that time. From those talks it has shown me how many people there were who tried to help those threatened by the Nazis – in many different ways.' Barbara has attended some of the events that have taken place in the last year, since the publication of the book and performances (almost all private until now) of the documentary film, and has met quite a few of Nicky's 'children' and their families. 'It has been very interesting and moving for me and my own children to talk to them about their memories and lives. I've also learnt more about my father's family and his life than I'd ever known before.' I am glad that my probing into their family background has proved to be of interest – it was a risk I took.

I very soon recognised something distinctive in this unassuming, apparently easygoing man I had met almost out of the blue. I was puzzled as to how a deed, requiring courage and a degree of audacity, with a remarkable outcome, could be wiped from one's memory. Whilst he had not *forgotten* the events of 1939 he had voluntarily or involuntarily put them to the back of his mind. His children do remember occasional references to their father's past experiences, but this particular episode would be passed off with the comments, 'It was all so long ago' or 'I do have the papers somewhere'. There must have been a great deal of pain experienced during those nine months.

Earlier this year I learnt about Sir Ronald Campbell, Ambassador to Lisbon in 1940, who, like our hero, had helped to save the live of 1,000 or more Jews. He died in 1953 without ever having told his family about his heroism. Unlike Nicky, he never had the experience of meeting any of those children he saved. Unlike Nicky, he was not recognised in his lifetime – the evidence, and there is a great deal of it – remains in the archives. I found that sad, but I doubt that Sir Ronald gave thought to the extent and outcome of his actions during his lifetime.

It was after the book was published, that I began to give thought to the context of the time at which the rescue mission took place. This important detail plus Winton's prescience distinguishes him from the cluster of well-known rescuers such as Schindler and Wallenberg whose admirable and amazing feats were accomplished in a completely different climate – a climate of mass deportations, deprivation and ultimate carnage. Winton arrived in Prague at the end of December 1938 – only three months after Munich – just six weeks since *Kristallnacht*. Certainly at this time Jews were being humiliated, degraded, excluded from many professions – their businesses, synagogues, houses attacked – they were disappearing and some died under

the stringent anti-Jewish laws in countries within the Third
Reich (Germany, Austria and the Sudetenland), but in scores,
even hundreds, not thousands. There were no extermination
camps at this time – not yet. Hitler's policy was emigration, not
extermination – not yet. The blueprint for the Final Solution
planned at Wannsee in early 1942 was still three years away. It
was May 1940 before Hitler was to conquer Holland and
Belgium and, finally, France. First deportations to the East took
place in October 1941. The massacres in Eastern Europe began
only after the Nazi invasion of the USSR in June 1941. Our story
takes place in the relative calm before the storm. So how was it
that he not only saw the danger, but acted and achieved?

Albert Camus (1913–60), the existentialist writer and philoso-
pher who lived through these times, pondered on the subject of
heroism and wondered if ordinary people do extra-ordinary
things merely out of simple decency.

I don't know that I am any the wiser now that I have written
down the details of his life – was it not, as I believe, an act of
pure decency?

Muriel Emanuel
December 2002

Introduction (II) to the Third Edition

When *Nicholas Winton and the Rescued Generation* was first published in November 2001, I was delighted with the positive response of the media and the public and with the ensuing requests for giving talks. The appreciation of the Winton children – particularly the new members of the clan – for giving them back part of their history by documenting what is in essence their story was very gratifying, but not as meaningful as the reaction of some members of the second generation.

'You have helped me open the door into my rich Czech past,' wrote Richard, who after the death of his father came to see me from Canada. 'I really appreciate all that you have done over the years. You, and now your book, are undoubtedly beacons for many like myself who have looked for information on a past that doesn't have much to give…'

'Unlike my late dad', wrote London-based Simon:

> I am not a great reader, but I was unable to put the book down and have read it from cover to cover in just two days – something of a record for me … Nicky Winton seems such a modest man, and I am glad that you have publicised what he did for the world. He undoubtedly gave dad an extra 60 years of life, and in June he will have given me 50 years. I have two brothers, a sister and two nephews. In my family alone these lives are owed to Nicholas, and yet there are 688 others! The echoes of his actions continue to be heard…In July, we had the stone-setting ceremony at my

father's grave. The following famous quotation from Edmund Burke has been engraved on his headstone: 'For evil to triumph all that is required is for good men to do nothing'. Whenever dad mentioned the quotation he thought of Nicky Winton. When so many other good people did nothing, Nicky did something. He made a difference.

On 25 September 2002, during the New Europe Film Festival at the Barbican, Simon and his brother Jonathan attended the London premier of Matej Mináč's documentary, *Nicholas Winton: The Power of Good*. Simon recalls the occasion:

> With all the media interest it was not possible to talk to Nicholas, but we ended up in the lift together as we all left. I was able to introduce myself and Jonathan as two more of his 'grandchildren'. Just to stand next to him and say 'Thank you' meant such a lot – I am sure you understand more than anyone …

In September 2001, I accompanied Nicky and his family to attend both the Slovak and Czech premier of *The Power of Good*: first in Bratislava, then in Prague. These were grand occasions, with many eminent guests and Winton children present. In Bratislava we were received by President Schuster in the castle, and enjoyed the warm hospitality and a superb lunch at the residence of the British Ambassador, David Lyscom, and his wife, who later came with us to see the film.

Watching the story of Nicky's life, interwoven with impressive archive material and recollections of some of us – the Winton children – was an unforgettable, incredibly moving experience. The film is greatly enhanced by the presence of Joe Schlesinger, the renowned Canadian TV journalist and a Winton child, who is the narrator and guide throughout. The deep affection Joe and Nicky feel for each other is there for all to see.

When the film ended, there was absolute silence, followed by thunderous applause, and a standing ovation. It seems that in the eyes of many this documentary rises above most films of its kind, because it is so personal, almost intimate; in other words, it has a heart. I felt proud that the manuscript of this book was instrumental in the making of Matej's film and that, in a small way, I had been involved in its production. I was touched by a letter written by Patrik Pass, Matej's co-producer, on behalf of them both, ending with the words, 'I am convinced that without your help and support we could never have achieved a result of such high quality and would not have earned such a positive response from the public.'

At the end of that memorable day there was a reception in Nicky's honour and, to my surprise, also to celebrate the launch of the Slovak edition of *Pearls of Childhood*. David Lyscom enjoyed dousing the very first book with champagne! This was, in a way, appropriate, as my autobiography had led Matej to me and the idea of the documentary was born. And now, at last, I was seeing the wonderful results.

Our stay in Prague and Bratislava took place during the fateful week of 11 September, when the world and the future irrevocably changed. The terrible happenings of that day were on everyone's mind, yet made Matej's film even more meaningful. I firmly believe that in today's troubled world when acts of terrorism and mass destruction of lives are on the daily menu, as is the uncertainty and fear of what lies ahead, highlighting the deeds of good, ordinary men who achieved extraordinary goals, gives a glimmer of hope. Nicky is an inspiration to us all. These sentiments were echoed in Prague by the American Ambassador, Craig Stapleton, who was at the première with his wife, Debbie. He told us that to begin with, he felt he should not attend, as his country was in mourning, but then he decided that now it was more important than ever to honour and applaud Nicky Winton, whose aim was to save lives, not to destroy them.

The ambassador and his wife have been good friends of Nicky ever since. They met up again this July in Prague and at the International Film Festival in Karlovy Vary (Carlsbad). Throughout the year *The Power of Good* has featured in various countries at many festivals; wherever shown, it won acclaim and awards. Nicky's fame spread, his popularity grew and with it the interest in our book (hence, the necessity for the second edition!) Nicky travelled to most of the major events, such as the premiere at the Simon Wiesenthal Center in Los Angeles, held on 9 April, the US Holocaust Remembrance Day. His daughter, Barbara, and granddaughter, Holly, were with him. In September, the New York premiere took place in the Symphony Space theatre, packed with around 9,000 spectators, many Winton children and dignitaries among them. Again, this unassuming man, who appears to take everything in his stride and whose sharp mind and exceptional energy makes him a youngster among us – his children – won everyone's hearts; even the hearts of Bill and Hilary Clinton, who Nicky met at a special reception. This was a most memorable visit. He was entertained royally, and was able to spend time with his American-based children and to get to know the new additions to the clan.

During Nicky's absence, I was inundated with requests for interviews with us, both by the British and foreign media, as shortly after his return the UK premiere of *The Power of Good* was to take place at the London Barbican cinema. The film had been selected to represent Slovakia during the New Europe Film Season. Thus, Nicky hardly had time to recover from his eventful trip before he was besieged again. There was coverage on all main British TV channels, also on Sky News and CNN. The telephone was still ringing as we were whisked off to the Barbican.

Prior to the film being shown, Peter Hain, formerly Minister for Europe, presented Nicky with a letter of recognition from the Prime Minister. This was a well-deserved tribute, but it made me wonder if Tony Blair was aware what an exceptional man Nicky is to this day. Shouldn't he be honoured also for his lifelong humanitarian activities, for his enormous contribution to the community? Even now, at the age of 93, he has raised over £1,000,000 to build another Extra Care Abbeyfield Home for the aged. How many men of his age can boast of such a feat?

The day after the London premiere, I flew to Prague to publicise the recently published Czech version of this book and also to visit my home town, Celakovice, with my sister Eva, who had come all the way from New Zealand to join my for a very special ceremony. The house, in which we had spent our short-lived childhood, and the medley of buildings behind it that had housed father's business, belonged to the town, but had been neglected for the past 60 years and were very dilapidated. Now all the buildings had been demolished and rebuilt in a most elegant style. It is, without doubt, the prettiest corner of our town, which, as a tribute to our family, the town council have renamed, 'At the Diamants'. At the side of the large ceramic plaque that hangs above the entrance and bears our family name, is a plaquette which states: 'Here stood the house in which the Diamant family lived. Their daughters, Vera and Eva, were rescued by the British citizen, Nicholas Winton. Their fate is documented in literature and film.'

As I stood in the courtyard packed with local people, listening to the mayor speaking so movingly about our family and our achievements, I felt as if our parents were there with us. They gave us life, and Nicky gave us a second chance of life; now their names are united – they will be remembered. (A new bookshop is part of the complex. It was crammed with the recently published book on Nicky. I spent over an hour signing each copy; it was an absolute sell-out.)

At the moment, another documentary is being prepared by Esther Rantzen, who has a special interest in Nicky's story, as back in February 1988 she introduced Nicky to millions of viewers and hundreds of 'his' children. As her film will concentrate mainly on the fate of the Winton children, it should be very compatible with Matej's. This time, I decided to take a back seat, but my contacts, and this book which contains so many varied stories of Nicky's extended family, have been a great asset to her.

I could hardly believe the fantastic news when I heard, towards the end of November, that *The Power of Good* had won the International Emmy Award for the best film in the television documentary category, out of more than 1,000 documentaries submitted from all over the world (except America). This prestigious award, which is also called 'the television Oscar', was presented to Matej on 25 November at the International Emmy Awards Gala at the Sheraton Hotel in New York City. It is the highest award any television film can receive.

What a proud moment it must have been for Matej – the culmination of his dreams! It was also a proud moment for me and my co-author, Muriel, because our book goes hand in hand with the film, and the film's success will help to promote the book. As for Nicky, pleased as he is with the outcome, he takes everything in his stride. When I told him that in the States, and in the Czech and Slovak Republic, he has now become a national hero and that I was concerned that he might be bombarded with demands for interviews and appearances, he said, 'Don't worry, I've got used to it – in fact, I rather like it; life would be so dull, so empty without all that...'

I am sad to add, that on the day we were celebrating Matej's achievements, Karel Reisz, the well-known film director who features in the film and in our book, has passed away after a long illness. The list of the children who are no longer with us is getting longer and longer. On the other hand, through the book and the film, new members keep on appearing. And we must not forget that most of us have children, grandchildren, even great-grandchildren; more than 5,000 of us would not be here today without Nicky's intervention.

For fourteen years I did my best to publicise Sir Nicholas Winton's story; thus for me the year 2002 could not have ended on a happier note. My delight that at long last his greatest achievement has been recognised by this country by the award of a knighthood is shared by the hundreds of his 'children' whom he has saved. Nicky gave us, our children and our grandchildren the chance of life.

Vera Gissing
January 2003

PART ONE

by Muriel Emanuel

1 Nicholas Winton: The Man

Nicholas Wertheim was born on 19 May 1909 in a house of some 20 rooms in West Hampstead. His paternal grandparents, Nicholaus (1836–1919) and Charlotte (née Kahn, born 1846), had settled in the United Kingdom at some point after their marriage in 1866, originally in Manchester. They later moved to London purchasing their Hampstead house in the 1870s. Nicholaus, who was born in Hanau, worked in the city and became a British citizen in 1868.

Their son Rudolph, Winton's father, married Barbara Wertheimer, who came from Nürnberg, in 1907. They settled in the family house and soon adapted to the ways of upper middle-class English London life, both professionally and socially.

There had been a considerable influx of young German Jews, many of them merchant bankers and stock brokers, arriving in London during the second half of the nineteenth century to find new lives and fortunes in the city. Few of them married English girls and those who did tended to marry into the upper classes, even the aristocracy.

These young men had trained in family merchant banks in their native cities, but London was considered the hub of the banking world and a period spent in the city would offer experience valuable to their future careers whether or not they returned to Germany.

For many of them, the decision to remain in London was

based on various factors. They enjoyed what the city had to offer and, above all, as Jews, felt secure in Britain. In some cases there may have been an awareness, even at this early stage, that the future for Jews in Germany could be risky.

Hampstead had become a nucleus for these well-educated, intellectual and highly ambitious families, originally from Germany, the majority retaining their Jewish, in some cases orthodox, identities. They associated almost exclusively with each other, having immense pride in their German heritage, but also a great warmth and respect for their adoptive country. The Wertheims (who did not change their name until 1938), lived within this community, but made a conscious decision to have their children baptised and brought up as Christians.

At the outbreak of World War I, Rudolf was not allowed to join a fighting force (although the son of naturalised parents), but served in a home-based regiment; he changed his name to Wertham for the duration of the war. On demobilisation he did not return to banking; he went into business and became a partner in a company dealing with Bohemian glass imported from Czechoslovakia.

* * *

Maternal antecedents came from Nürnberg, a mediaeval city where Jews had first settled as early as the twelfth century, but were tolerated by the local rulers only if they lived in approved areas and paid the heavy taxes demanded of them. There were many pogroms, in 1349 as many as 500 Jews died, and there were many expulsions, the last 'for all time', in 1498, left the city without Jews for 350 years.

Known for Dürer, who lived and worked there, and associated with Wagner's *Die Meistersinger*, Nürnberg became the centre for Nazi rallies and gave its name to the despicable racist laws of the 1930s.

Although Jews had not been permitted to live within the city for more than three centuries, a solid community had built up in nearby Fürth from where numerous families came at the time of the resettlement. The decision to allow their return in 1850 was taken with the intention of improving the economic situation and it would seem that Sigmund Wertheimer (Winton's grandfather) was amongst the early resettlers. It is possible that the family came originally from Wertheim, in Bavaria, but this cannot be corroborated. From these years until the establishment of the Weimar Republic following World War I, Nürnberg was not known for anti-Semitism. An industrial city, with many small businesses, the Jewish population thrived and important positions in all sections of the community were held by Jews.

Winton's grandfather held a responsible position with the municipality and was awarded a 'citizen's medal'. A relatively prosperous family, the Wertheimers had a comfortable life and were well respected within the general community. They felt secure and were extremely patriotic. Sigmund and his wife, Mathilda Lust, had five children. With the exception of Winton's mother, who settled in London after her marriage in 1907, they remained in Germany until the Nazi threat became palpable.

The Wertheimers were a highly educated and academic family. Winton's mother, Barbara, was born in Nürnberg in 1888; she had been the first girl to pass Abitur (matriculation) in Germany. Two of her siblings, Dr Ida McAlpine and Dr Fredric Wertham, were to become eminent in the field of psychiatry.

A lively, attractive young girl, with an outstanding mind, she was quite unsuited to a conventional domestic family life and could not have savoured the surroundings presented to her on arrival in London in 1907. She was not attracted to the lifestyle of the German émigré families living nearby, most of whom respected their Jewish ancestry, if only tenuously. The months leading up to and the duration of World War I were a period of intense anti-German feeling. The family was ostracised; the few friends she had made would not speak to her until after the armistice in 1918. She may have felt overshadowed by the academic successes of her siblings and possibly trapped in her domestic environment. She developed a degree of bitterness and discontentment, thus creating a frustration that revealed a haughty exterior which did not inspire friendship. She was by no means without warmth, as shown when dealing with the problems of the children saved by her son.

Winton remembers his mother's very positive outlook on life. She found herself unable to suffer those with little intellectual knowledge or interest; she was even hard on her family in this respect. Her Jewish background played little importance in her life or the life of her family, but to deny her heritage would have seemed childish and a waste of time. She had Jewish friends and often used untranslatable 'Jewish' (probably Yiddish) words or phrases. She did, after all, choose to stay in an area of London where there was a large, active Jewish community.

Of her three children, Nicholas was her favourite. No girlfriend was ever good enough in her eyes and she did not approve of his choice of bride, Grete, from Denmark, with whom Nicholas had a loving and enriching relationship for over 50 years.

Once war had been declared in September 1939, after which Winton was no longer able to get children out of Prague, he felt there was no more he could do – his 'job' was done. A committed pacifist at the time, he felt unable to enlist, but was anxious to play his part in defeating the Nazis, whose inhuman behaviour he had already witnessed at first hand. He joined the Red Cross and was soon sent to France as a volunteer ambulance driver. At this time, his mother made herself available to any of the children needing after-care, but only a handful of the children knew of her existence. Those who did contact her with their problems found her warm and sympathetic; emotions that did not come easily to her. She died at the age of 91 in a home for the elderly in north-west London.

Dr Ida McAlpine, his mother's sister, was Winton's favourite aunt. As a teenager he admired her and loved to be with her. She arrived in the United Kingdom in 1933 and reached great eminence as a psychoanalyst. Together with her son, Dr Richard Hunter, she produced the book *Three Hundred Years of Psychiatry 1535–1860* (Oxford University Press, 1963) which remained the standard reference work for many years. Her book, *George III and the Mad Business* (Allen Lane, 1969) revolutionised public and professional thinking on the actions of the king; his symptoms appeared to relate to porphyria rather than a mental state. The book was the major reference for Alan Bennett when researching his play *The Madness of George III*, presented at the National Theatre, London, in 1992 with Ida McAlpine as a character in the production. It was later made into a film.

EARLY DAYS: 1909–31

Nicholas Winton is that archetype product of the twentieth-century English public-school system: reserved, gentlemanly and beautifully mannered. A façade, but never a mask, that belies his background, for there is nothing hidden in his nature, although in time I came to feel that his Jewish ancestry was somewhat of an embarrassment, or maybe something hard for him to believe. He could not understand when I explained to him that, in Jewish law, he was considered a Jew despite his baptism and that he would not have escaped had the Nazi regime succeeded in occupying the United Kingdom. According to *Halacha* (Jewish law) a child born of a Jewish mother, who herself has a Jewish mother, is without exception and in all circumstances a Jew. He was always aware of his background, but the details remained hazy. 'There I was,' he said, 'meeting the family's Jewish friends, but not really being accepted by them, being not of their faith, and being treated with suspicion by my Christian acquaintances for having a German/Jewish name.' His parents did not intentionally keep him ignorant of the details of his family background; he was never sufficiently interested to enquire.

He was five when World War I began and can remember the zeppelin raids and going down to the cellar of their Hampstead home, wrapped in blankets, whilst bombs fell on the railway line near Belsize Park. At that age, it seemed a lot of fun and it was many years later that Winton came to realise the anguish and difficulties his parents must have experienced at that time. It was barely seven years since his mother had arrived in London; she was going through a hard time – she was lonely. So many of her new friends had deserted her as anti-German feeling was high and she was constantly concerned about her family in Germany – the hated enemy.

As a boarder at Stowe and from the end of 1939 until the

disclosure of the story of the *kindertransports* in 1988 (well over half his life), Winton had little contact with Jews. As a small child and later at day school in Hampstead, the presence of the local Jewish families would never have been questioned.

During his formative years, growing up in Hampstead, it seems his parents' friends were from backgrounds similar to their own. On the one hand, having had their children baptised, they appeared to want to leave their Jewish faith behind them; on the other hand, having chosen to live in the house purchased by Winton's grandparents deep in the heart of prosperous 'Jewish London', it would have been difficult to make a complete break.

In Hamburg and Berlin in the late 1920s and early 1930s when he was training in the banks of these cities, he would find himself accepting hospitality from well-to-do Jewish families. On a Friday night in June 1929 he visited the Meyer family where there were three elderly ladies, he presumed to be family, and two other guests. He noted in his diary:

> Before dinner there was a small Jewish ceremony and later on, one of the men, a Zionist, discorted (*sic*) on the Jews all over the world. Apparently they all thought I was Jewish so I tactfully put them right ... we had a fine dinner which was alone worth going for.

The Meyers continued to invite him on Friday nights 'despite the last episode on a Friday evening ... Herr Meyer said prayers as usual ... we talked, or rather they talked, until 11 when I was able to escape'. It was probably a sense of duty and the good food that made him accept these invitations, but maybe he was less uncomfortable in these surroundings than he likes to remember. He was introduced to girls by the Meyers and they went on drives and picnics together. In October he 'went round to the Meyers to wish them a Happy New Year and take flowers'.

After 1988 Winton developed very special relationships with a number of the children he had saved, but he has never felt an identity with or a kinship to Jewish people. He has a great feeling for family unity and has always been prepared to embrace people for what they are and not for what they were born. Vera Gissing had no idea of his background and was only made aware of his ancestry some time after their first meeting and then by accident; she found it hard to believe. Of his German heritage, either in appearance, language or manner, there is barely a trace. His German is fluent, though with an English accent.

Many of the major merchant banking families in Britain can be found to have similar backgrounds: German, often Jewish (sometimes baptised), public school and Oxbridge, or, as in Winton's case, the city, becoming well established and respected in the community. So what *does* make him unique? He never became socially ambitious – he had no desire to climb higher in the social hierarchy and felt thoroughly relaxed in whatever environment he took on board during his extremely diverse life. Perhaps it was his adaptability, unusual, at least at that time, amongst those with such a rarefied and privileged upbringing, that set him further apart from his peers.

By the time Nicholas Winton was born in 1909, countless German-Jewish men, many of them bankers and stockbrokers, had come to try their luck in the important banking centre of London, many making their homes in Hampstead. Together with their German-born wives, they brought up their families in large comfortable houses similar to that of the Wertheims. Although, at this time, Winton's parents had no intention of changing their name, they had made a conscious decision to leave their Judaism behind. Their adoption, if it could be called such, of Christianity hardly went further than the baptism of their children. The boys had to attend chapel at school and were confirmed. Their choice to stay in Hampstead, where so many other ex-patriots resided, demonstrated their wish not to divorce themselves entirely from their background. Although Winton's parents spoke perfect English, they made a point of speaking German at home – they wanted their children to be familiar with both languages.

Nicholas went to University College School; his German name and German-Jewish background, but Christian upbringing, resulted in a dichotomy and in some respects was

9

socially isolating; however, Winton cannot recall any problems with anti-Semitism. His best friend during the years at preparatory school was Stanley Murdoch, indeed this friendship was to last until Murdoch's death; Winton is godfather to both Murdoch's daughter and granddaughter.

Winton had a strong desire to be part of the English public-school system and when his friend went on to Stowe in 1923, soon after the foundation of the school, he persuaded his parents to be allowed to join him. He was 14 and began as a boarder. He has told me that his memories of those years are not happy, particularly the first term, but when, some time later, I came across his diaries, I found no reference to his misery. Just a sad little note in his diary of 1925 – on the first page, under Memoranda, together with the times of his extra Latin lessons and confirmation classes: 'I want to be happy.' Winton made few friends amongst the rather snobbish upper middle-class boys, but how much was because of the unfamiliar atmosphere can only be presumed. He was certainly not good at cricket which did not go down at all well, but he took up fencing at which he excelled.

A rapport developed between Winton and his maths teacher, Heckstall-Smith, who had a great influence on him and brought life into the subject. When he left Stowe and was considering a career in the city, he recalled the confidence inspired by his teacher and never found the banking world dull.

At Stowe light is thrown on the prominence of sport and the Officers' Training Corps, with its weekly drill and gun practice, on which Winton is none too keen. Unlike most of the boys, he dreads camp and is bad at shooting. Possibly, the seeds of his pacifism are sown at this time. Cricket, rugger, boxing and cross-country running were all intensely competitive, either within the school or against other schools. It is in fencing that he really shines and to which he is truly committed; he idolises his teacher, Captain Felix Gravé, who had taught his father and who tells Winton: 'I will make a good fencer out of you.' Indeed he did.

It is obvious that family ties are strong, with consistent visits to Stowe, but his parents seldom visit together, his father often being tied up with business. For his birthday, Winton noted,

'Father gave me some books ... Mother gave me some links' and 'Mother sent me a telegram and father sent me a letter'. He is intensely proud of his family when they attend sports and open days; his attractive and elegant mother, his impeccably mannered father. Precisely which members of the family are present at these events are noted as well as the gifts received from each one of them. He expresses disappointment if an expected visit is postponed, or a letter fails to arrive, but this seldom happens. He notes each time he receives letters and reprimands his mother if she is tardy in writing to him.

His feelings are rarely mentioned, but when one of his pet pigeons dies he writes 'I am very sad about it', and on a holiday in Belgium after the family had visited the battlefields he writes, 'very interesting, but terribly sad – we went to hill 60 – it was terrible'.

During the holidays he plays chess with his father and billiards and table tennis with friends, of which there never seemed to be a shortage. Stanley Murdoch is the most constant visitor. There must have been a well-equipped games room in the house. He watches his parents, mostly his mother, and their friends play bridge. He accompanies his mother on endless shopping expeditions to Harrods, or 'to Bradley's to see Ma's new coat', or to tea at Gunters. Life is totally family orientated with outings to the cinema and theatre. *Grossmama* seems to supply his more intellectual needs and when visiting from Berlin takes him to the Tate Gallery which he finds 'rather boring' and introduces him to Shakespeare which he loves.

In August 1925 the family are packing for their four-week holiday in Belgium. 'Pa is not coming with us', he writes, without expressing regret or otherwise.

On return from holiday Winton spends time with his father 'I met father in the city – he ordered me three new evening shirts'. Winton is 16 at this time and enjoying life. He begins to go to dances, mostly in private houses and his sister, Lottie, is sent to Switzerland. His mother asks if he wants to go to Switzerland, but, he writes, 'I don't want to leave Ma, etc.' One wonders at the significance of the 'etc.' and is inclined to believe that there could be strains at home. Certainly never a moment is

11

left free and most pastimes and outings seem to involve the family, particularly his mother. When they are not occupied with various games, they are at the cinema, theatre, or opera or out shopping, having tea or dinner out, or they 'go for drives' – his mother driving their newly acquired motor car.

Winton sees mouthwatering performances – Sybil Thorndike's Lady Macbeth and *Tristan und Isolde* with Lauritz Melchior and Freda Leider, 'one of the most beautiful operas I have heard'. There are constant visitors and it is interesting to note that almost without exception, his family's friends are German ex-patriots and mostly Jewish: a luxurious and expensive life, always on the go.

On his return to school for the spring term in 1926, Winton is not happy. He finds the work very hard; he keeps pigeons as pets and becomes very attached to them; he writes copious letters, mostly to the family and to each one separately.

His mixed background continued to be invasive throughout his student days and early working life. At Stowe it was presumed he would be confirmed at 16, but he requested time to consider the matter. He felt the moment had come to make decisions concerning his place in society. He felt 'torn in two' and asked himself 'where do I belong?'. He had no grounding in either Christianity or Judaism; he knew a little more about the former which he had learnt at school, but had no depth of knowledge. About Judaism he was totally ignorant and had no particular interest, nor was he encouraged to learn more about this part of his background. Even this questioning, minor though it was, was not understood by either of his siblings. Having delayed his confirmation for a year, he came to the decision that he would embrace Christianity, not so much in a religious sense, but as a social identity; he made a decision to marry a Christian girl. He mentions none of these thoughts in his diary writings.

On the day, 'Mother, Father and Bobby came down to my confirmation. We had tea in assembly after the service. Pa and Ma gave me a lovely watch and Grandma gave me a pound. They are staying overnight.' The following day he goes to communion and 'got on very well'. He continues to attend church throughout his time at Stowe seldom mentioning the content of the sermons – they were either good or not so good. He does not become a regular churchgoer.

The diary ceases at the end of March and resumes at the beginning of 1927, by which time he has left Stowe and is ready to embark on his career. Having left without the required matriculation grades, he continued his studies at evening classes whilst serving an apprenticeship at the city bank during the day.

His father wished his son to follow in the footsteps of the family and go into banking, a career mapped out for him without consultation, but Winton was not against the idea. He did not have strong feelings for any other profession and with his aptitude for maths a career in the city seemed to make sense.

Winton is 18 in 1927 and the year begins with many dances, even one at the Wertheims; he takes dancing lessons and learns the Charleston. After a 'simply wonderful' performance of *Pygmalion*, he decides 'only to read good books. I am going to read a lot of Shawe (*sic*).' Besides Shaw, he reads Coleridge and becomes a member of a local library. He does not consider his weekly allowance of 6d. (2½p.) overgenerous, 'I shall have to be careful what I do'; he also receives a latchkey. Fencing continues to be his passion and his lessons with Captain Gravé which continue in London give him immense pleasure. Although not of a particularly competitive disposition, his mastery of the sport gives him confidence.

Winton occasionally attends church, sometimes with Stanley Murdoch; only once or twice during his time in Germany is a Sunday church service mentioned. He dislikes services which are 'too high church'. The diaries continue to be non-committal, but there is a suggestion that a degree of conflict may still lurk in his religious mind. He makes a point of attending a debate at Queens Hall on 'Life and Religion' and sometime later 'had a religious discussion with the two Lotty's (*sic*)', but maddeningly refrains from any comment on either of these incidents.

In February, Winton starts work in the city at the merchant bankers S. Japhet where he deals with the correspondence. His hours are from 9am to 6pm plus Saturday mornings and he receives a salary of £4 per month. On the very first day he writes in his diary: 'I don't know if I shall like it.' Winton has little contact with the partners, 'I have still not seen any of the bosses ... I am getting more mechanical.' He frequently meets his father in the city, during his lunch break, where they discuss city life and his progress at the bank. At this time he is very close to his father who is always supportive and encouraging: 'Father explains all I don't understand in the evening.' He sometimes swims and plays squash at the RAC where his father is a member. Rudi seems to have been a lonely man, very much in love with, but dominated by, his beautiful intelligent wife. He stands somewhat apart from the family; always there to make up numbers for bridge or a game of chess, but never able or encouraged to join in any fun. Drives to the country and picnics always seem to be without him, as are most outings to the cinema and theatre.

Winton takes a one month's course at Pitmans followed by private lessons in shorthand and typing; in order to keep up with the language, he writes to his grandmother in German.

One significant entry in March of this year gives a glimpse of Winton's humanism and his caring nature which will prevail 12 years on. His close friend, Stanley Murdoch, troubled by the strain of his parents' relationship, culminating in their divorce two years later, expresses the desire to get a caravan and some books and live alone. Winton is shocked, 'I explained this was running away from the world and not doing his share in the community'. Winton continues with his own thoughts, 'He apparently does not understand that although he is running away from the world he is still dependent on the community.' These words bring a breath of fresh air into what appears to be a round of sybaritic pleasures in the highly material world surrounding Winton both at work and at home, where values seem to be based on the power that wealth brings.

By March 'work in the office is beginning to get a little "flat", but I hope to be able to find some fresh land to conquer soon'. By April he is fed up with his diary and gives up. There is no diary for 1928, or if there was, it has been destroyed. He gets going again in 1929 where one of his early entries describes his attempt to smoke a pipe 'to give one a certain amount of self

14

confidence and makes conversation easy. However, I have a tongue like leather from it.'

Despite the gloom in the city, the round of parties and dances proceed, going on until the early hours; the Thames freezes and there are many opportunities to skate that winter. In the midst of these jollities there is another caring diary entry, 'It is still well below freezing and parts of the community are suffering badly.'

Winton could not wait for the visit of his Aunt Ida. Divorced from Ernst Hirschman, her husband of three years, she had left her two sons Karl and Richard 'to whom she has already explained where they come from', with her mother in Berlin.

> We talked, or rather Auntie Ida did, until midnight … Auntie Ida is wonderful. She talks like a steam engine, but it is all perfectly good sense, she radiates happiness although she is unwell. I think she is very pleased to be here.

When Ida leaves after two weeks, to attend a medical conference in Wiesbaden, Winton notes in his diary 'Ma is very sad.'

Barbara must have been envious of Ida's success and independence and felt low after her visit. Her life seemed humdrum, her intelligence and talents wasted. She did not consider the advantages of a stable home life with children of any value. This mood did not last and she threw herself back into a hectic social life and devoted attention to her children.

Winton begins to mention girls (he is 19) and in particular Elizabeth who is 17, 'I think she is pretty and certainly interesting'. Elizabeth O'Malley has a truly romantic background – orphaned when she was very young she is in the care of a Mr Sala who seems wealthy and kind, as is her governess who is in attendance whenever Winton and Elizabeth get together.

> We had a family evening. It has now been definitely decided that I shall go away for a holiday in May and start in the bank in Hamburg in June. I shall very likely stay there for a year and then go on to Paris and then to New York.

15

It did not occur to Winton to question decisions made by his father. Several years abroad to gain experience in international banking appealed to him.

He says his goodbyes to friends and family, with true German reverence, including a visit to Stowe (with Elizabeth and governess). 'I shall be sorry to leave Elizabeth as we have got very friendly in a very short time and three years of correspondence – well – perhaps I can?' He finishes at Japhets in April:

> I am not at all sorry to leave, although I made many friends and they were all always very good to me. As things stand now, I shall be back there in three years. I wonder – and if so what position!

On 20 May he leaves for Berlin with his mother. They are met by his sister Lottie and one of Ida's sons at the station from where they go to *Grossmama*'s apartment which is 'wonderful – just what I would like for myself (when married)'. They visit countless relatives, but most of all, he loves to be in the company of his Aunt Ida. He goes with her when she visits patients and walks around while she is working. They go to the opera together and see *The Marriage of Figaro*. His father arrives and they make excursions together, but soon it is time to get him settled in Hamburg, 'The thought of the city again away from home is none too pleasant.'

Barbara's youngest brother, Paul, is living in Hamburg at this time and meets them at the station. During his year in Hamburg Winton sees his uncle two or three times each week, frequently having lunch or dinner with him, taking walks, going on expeditions into the country and visiting Paul's friends. Although always referred to as Uncle Paul, Winton is only nine years younger, and they enjoy each other's company. Paul considers him well informed and intelligent, but does not hesitate to reprimand him if he considers he is playing too hard and not studying enough. I suspect that he did not have the social privileges available to his nephew.

Winton's father accompanies his son to the bank, Behrens

und Soehne, to meet Dr Eberstadt, presumably the senior partner. His diary entry on that day, 'I don't think I have said a word for a few days', gives a picture of this young man of 20 still under the control of his overprotective parents who are also determined to find suitable rooms for their son in an environment that meets with their approval. Winton himself is more concerned about the long working day (9.00am–1pm and 3.00–7.00pm).

He moves in with Herr and Frau Valk who live on the outskirts of the town – a 25-minute journey by tram to the bank, which enables him to go home for lunch. His parents leave for London: 'A very sad parting.'

The Valk family befriend him and include him in family outings; their maid, 18-year-old Gretschen, helps him with his German when they go on long walks together. But in August he is 'fed up with the Valks and thinking of changing rooms'. This comes to nothing and must have been a momentary mood change. He comes to the conclusion that other rooms would be more expensive and 'without the advantages', what advantages he does not define. Perhaps the Valks were too effusive with their hospitality and protective feelings. The taking of such decisions still had to be referred to family: 'I have written home and I must wait and see what they say.'

His diary entries are preoccupied with his correspondence. 'I wrote a most sentimental letter home ... wrote letter in the evening ... no letters yet. It is about time Elizabeth wrote' and at last 'received three letters from Ma who expressed her feeling about our parting in a very nice letter'.

Another preoccupation is his health. The least sniff is entered, a sore throat, his temperature and times spent in bed or housebound, a wound from fencing or the boat, the medicines prescribed. He takes good care of himself.

Winton quickly builds up a social life in Hamburg as busy as that in London. Introductions from home result in invitations to dinner parties, dances, the theatre and, much to his delight, the opera, where he is impressed with the standard in what is essentially a provincial town. *Tannhauser* (with Melchior), *Die Meistersinger*, *Tosca*, *Die Fledermaus* (produced by Max Reinhart),

17

The Ring, 'three super Wagners in one week', always in a box or the best seats (when invited), but up in the balcony when paying for himself. It is not difficult to find bridge partners or people to go on walks with. 'It's curious how everyone here has the nack (*sic*) to make themselves agreeable', he writes, but there are times when he is inhibited by the more aggressive type of young men who come his way: 'L has got a nice room in Schlup, but as far as I can see we will not have much to do with each other. I am too tame for him and he is too much of a vulgar lout for me.' L's father is a director of one of the largest banks in Hamburg.

Of the actual work which involves him at the bank, he writes little, but in August he starts work in the Document Department which he finds interesting and instructive. By October work is beginning to slacken and he does not have enough to do; he now leaves the office by 6.00pm.

His interest in sailing grows and he becomes part owner of a boat. Life is full and he feels comfortable in Hamburg 'until I think of home ... I myself am happy, but the only thing that makes me a little sad is the thought they might be sad at home'. Again, does this infer a strained relationship between his parents?

His epistolary romance with Elizabeth seems to flourish. 'My correspondence with Elizabeth is going strong and we have now corresponded for a longer time than we have actually known each other in London.'

Winton continues with his fencing, but finds the standard less good than in London: 'the professional is nowhere near as good as Captain Gravé'. He is asked to fence for Hamburg against Copenhagen, but needs to ask his father for extra cash and the office for time off, both of which are forthcoming. The match takes place in Heiligendamm, the Danes proving far superior to the Hamburg team and they lost all but one of their fights. Fencing every week becomes too expensive, but he is lucky to be offered honorary guest membership of the Hamburger Fechtklub, who do not usually admit foreigners, whereby he gets lessons from the *meister* for which he pays 30 Reichmarks every three months.

At this time there are diary entries in German. He has become extremely fluent and one presumes that he is now speaking German all the time. In November he starts a course at the University Theoretische Sozialokonomie under Professor Sieveking and decides to cut down on his social life and late nights.

Home for Christmas, with a round of parties. His disappointment on finding Elizabeth away in Paris is alleviated by her return in time for the New Year when he 'danced all the time with E at the Dragon, a small club behind the Coliseum – very select – actors, actresses – Mr Sala just sat!' His romance flourished at the respectable level expected in those days. Winton was presumably accepted by Mr Sala as a presentable and reliable suitor for his ward as they had several unchaperoned meetings, but no more is heard of Elizabeth after the diary entries of 1929.

Back in Hamburg early in the New Year his diary entries become sporadic. Dorothy and Margot Heinemann[1] are in Hamburg and he sees them regularly, particularly Dorothy. But the mood is grim 'more and more people are being sacked in the office and the outlook is exceedingly black ... first floor staff are being moved down and that floor will be let ... business is very bad and the policy of the banks is to do as little as possible'. There are now only 80 employees out of the 160 who were there at the time of his arrival less than a year ago.

His time in Hamburg is coming to an end, as are his diary entries. On 22 April he moves to Berlin where he finds rooms in Mommsenstrasse. He pays his first visit to the Stock Exchange which he finds 'very thrilling'.

In Berlin, Winton works for Wassermanns, merchant bankers, and enjoys a grand life with his own boat on the Wannsee and opportunities to practise his fencing. These months were amongst the happiest of his youth enjoying the good life as an impecunious apprentice on the periphery of the 'grand set'.

Uninvolved with politics at this time and within the cocoon of the banking world, he was not aware of the ugly incidents occurring around him. He did not seek them out. The environment wherein he worked was stimulating; every moment was full. Hitler had already been on the scene for some years, but was still not taken seriously by the people with whom Winton was mixing. Although Jews were well represented in banking in Germany at that time, such events were not part of his world. Jew baiting on any scale had not begun; Jewish families only spoke of the subject within the security of their own homes and were convinced it was 'a passing phase'.

There is some confusion as to when he left Berlin and went to work for the Banque Nationale de Credit in Paris where he remained until February 1931. Winton can recall few details of his time in this city.

It had been considered that a year in New York would round off his banking experience and qualify him for a good position almost anywhere in Europe, but circumstances in Germany at that time on two counts, the financial crisis and the rise of the Third Reich, caused him to change his plans; the good life came to an abrupt end in 1931.

America was recovering from the 1929 Wall Street collapse and the European economic situation was gloomy. Winton's father called him back to London. His intended year in New York was abandoned.

Now fluent in French and German and well acquainted with banking procedures, it was time to earn some money.

THE CITY: 1931–39

Winton returned to London in 1931 with every intention of making banking his lifetime career. In spite of having spent two years in Germany, he was not able to foresee the changing face of Europe nor the events of 1939 that would alter his life forever.

His first job was, ironically, with the Anglo-Czech Bank, but after three months, when the promised increase in his salary was not forthcoming, he complained to his boss and was promptly sacked! Orders had been received from Prague to cut costs. It was the early days of the depression and the city was playing carefully.

Winton did not remain unemployed for long and was soon

working for Ullman and Company. Now 22, he considered it high time to move out of the family home. With his old school friend, Stanley Murdoch, he rented a flat in Belsize Park. This lifelong friendship was of particular warmth and ease. Winton always had the feeling that Murdoch's parents did not find his family acceptable – they were probably confused by the German-Jewish name yet the Christian upbringing, and there was no doubt that Murdoch spent more time at the Wertheim home than the other way round, but Mrs Murdoch was always very kind to Winton.

Winton had always wanted to fly. He began taking lessons at Stag Lane, Hendon in North London, qualifying as a pilot in 1933. He met Amy Johnson and Jim Mollison who made the first flight across the Atlantic that year. Unfortunately, by the time he joined the Royal Air Force in 1942, his eyesight was too poor for him to qualify as a pilot.

At Ullmans he gained experience in all aspects of banking. He became a dealer and developed their Stock Exchange and Foreign Exchange activities. He remained with Ullmans until 1936 when he moved to Vanderfelts from where he was 'headhunted' to Crews and Company, the firm that was to show so little compassion with his work in Prague some years later. He was admitted as a Member of the London Stock Exchange in 1937 at a cost of £2,000.

That year he was sent to Johannesburg to open joint accounts for the company. A five-day journey by flying boat was the quickest way there. Champagne dinners and sightings from the air (very thrilling at that time) of St Peter's and Vesuvius and the ancient sites of Greece and Egypt. Travel was only possible in good weather and during daylight hours; consequently there were numerous stops, where tours were arranged; he visited places of great interest he would not otherwise have seen. A keen photographer, he returned to England with shots of enormous fish jumping out of the water, herds of elephants, hippopotami, buffaloes, bucks, gazelles and flamingoes by the hundred on Lake Lekuro, the only breeding ground in the world of the pink birds. On the flight from Naivasha to Mombasa they glimpsed the magnificent Mount Kilimanjaro peeping through the clouds. The 7,500 mile journey had been stupendous.

Winton enjoyed his years in the city. His various jobs in banking and stockbroking were sufficiently diverse and at times exciting. Life was never humdrum – he never permitted it to be so – he grasped every opportunity that came his way. He was successful and felt secure in his profession.

In 1938 he was chosen for selection to the British fencing team at the Olympics, but war intervened.

Never attracted to great wealth, 'I have not seen money make anyone happy, often the contrary ...', and not overly ambitious, Winton was always committed to the task he had undertaken. With no great personal demands, he managed a comfortable lifestyle, particularly after his marriage in 1948. It never concerned him when he was short of money and unable to do the more extravagant things he saw others do, but he was able to enjoy money when he had it. He never coveted riches and in his later years, when settled with his family in Berkshire, he never felt the need for more than was required to maintain his house and beloved garden. Greed and social ambition were not in his nature.

* * *

Although Winton was no longer living at his parents' house, he was aware of a strangeness within the family home at this time. A strangeness he could not understand and was unable to come to terms with. From the mid-1930s, relatives and friends of his parents, most of whom he hardly knew, began arriving at their Hampstead home. They were not like the visitors he was used to; they had very little baggage and did not bring presents. They came as refugees. Dispirited and helpless, they stayed with the Winton family until such time as they were able to find homes and work. Because he was not there all the time Winton did not hear the day-to-day conversations that must have taken place and at first he was able to stand apart from the agonies of these foreign relations and what was happening in Germany. There were still many people who believed it was a passing phase, but nevertheless their fear was palpable. Hitler was evil, but surely the German people were far too intelligent to allow such a man to control them? As time went on, however, Winton's curiosity was aroused and he began to be aware of the true situation and the danger facing the Jews.

Neville Chamberlain made his historic journey to Munich in 1938, returning waving a piece of paper and the sham 'Peace in our Time'. (*Kristallnacht* followed just five weeks later.) War clouds were, nonetheless, looming, but the atmosphere in the city was very pro-German and even then the threat of Hitler was not taken with any seriousness. Winton has said: 'If Hitler had arrived in Throgmorton Street in the late thirties he would have been as welcome as he was in Vienna at the time of the Anschluss.'

In an entirely different context, it was Martin Blake, his left-wing schoolmaster friend, who familiarised him with the ugly events going on in Germany and who foresaw a threat to the rest of Europe; together they attended meetings of the Peace Pledge Union in Sussex. Blake was friendly with Tom Driberg, Aneurin Bevan and Jennie Lee, all active socialists and later Labour members of parliament in the Atlee postwar team. Winton was introduced to this circle; he was fascinated by Bevan, his quick wit elevated any company he was part of and at that time engendered feelings of optimism. Winton also thought highly of Jennie Lee.

Another important influence on his political thinking was Maurice Lovell whom he met through his sister, Lottie. Lovell was working for the Ministry of Information at the time; later he was a Reuter's correspondent in Eastern Europe – in Romania and the USSR – where he had a distinguished career in journalism. Winton can never remember discussing politics with his family.

Life took a dramatic turn at this time; his sudden political maturity, or maybe the influence of the people he was meeting who seemed to be doing something to change the world, had the effect of making him feel the need to make his personal contribution. Sooner than he could have ever believed, an opportunity was to come his way.

He had, on a number of occasions, helped Blake on skiing expeditions to Switzerland accompanying a party of Westminster schoolboys. However, just before Christmas 1938 Blake asked Winton to cancel his bookings to Switzerland and come straightaway to Prague where he 'had something to show him'. Winton perceived a sense of urgency. He had two weeks' holiday due to him and was anxious to get there as soon as possible. He flew from Croydon on the next plane out.

These two weeks, with difficulty extended to three, were to change the direction of his life.

* * *

The story of the rescue mission is told by Vera Gissing in Chapter 2. I take up his life story at the declaration of World War II in September 1939.

DARK DAYS: 1939–45

The eight months Winton had devoted to the saving of the children had been a time of intense physical and emotional pressure. The pace at which he had worked had been all-consuming; the hours spent at the bank were simply cut-off times and the minute the Stock Exchange closed he had been back on the job.

To return to the mundane routine of the bank when the world so near to him was in turmoil was not an option. He made the decision to resign from the bank while still awaiting call-up.

The danger of German expansion was far more real to Winton than to most of the people with whom he came into contact through his work. He was 30 and at that time had no conflict with his pacifism, but he did feel the need to identify with the fight against the evils of fascism and in some way make his contribution to the war effort. He also felt a measure of disgust at the attitude prevailing in the city. His career was progressing well and his employers took a dim view of his decision to enlist. Their argument was that there would be money to be made and failed to understand why he found himself unable to take financial advantage of the situation. Even after the declaration of war there were members of the Stock Exchange who were unable to take the situation seriously and believed that it would all blow over in a short time.

Air raids had been expected, certainly on London. At 11.00am on Sunday 3 September 1939, silver barrage balloons rose into the sky and the sirens wailed within minutes of Chamberlain's speech on the BBC announcing that Great Britain was, from that moment, at war with Germany. For a second time that day the sirens sounded; people rushed to the shelters, brown cardboard boxes containing their gas masks over their shoulders, their anxiety and bewilderment disguised with jokes and *bonhomie*. These proved to be simple reconnaissance raids and the following months became known as the 'Phoney War' or 'Twilight War' as coined by Neville Chamberlain – the silence was uncanny. France was also free of air attacks during this time and the allies refrained from attacking Germany. Meanwhile Poland was strafed beyond belief and a great number of German U-boats were causing destruction and death at sea.

At the time of Munich, in September 1938, any shame felt by the sacrifice of Czechoslovakia was said to be mitigated by the fact that Great Britain was so ill-prepared for outright war. A year later, the situation was little changed. There were massive call-ups and non-stop and frantic training of the forces. The formation of a Home Guard of men over 40, most of whom had served in World War I, was suggested at this time, but not developed until May of the following year.

Two days before the declaration of hostilities, Winton was requested by the Ministry of Health to set up an ARP (Air Raid Precautions) depot in Hampstead. Expecting bombs to fall at any moment, but unable to envisage the requirements for dealing with damage and casualties, he was first instructed to get hold of as many vehicles as possible. Lorries and lifting gear to deal with damaged buildings would be needed as well as smaller cars to take the mobile wounded to hospitals, leaving the ambulances to take the more serious cases. The call went out for private cars, with instructions to pay no more than £5 per vehicle.

It was expected that petrol would not be available during the period of hostilities and there was no shortage of vehicles; at one time people were queueing up to sell their cars. The depot was set up with transport and gear and volunteers trained to deal with the expected emergencies. They sat and waited, drinking gallons of tea, playing interminable games of cards, listening to news bulletins over and over again, but the bombings failed to materialise and they became weary and frustrated. Extreme boredom was avoided by the music they were able to listen to and discuss, as many of the volunteers were musicians from the Royal Opera House and other London orchestras. The atmosphere was strange and unreal. Had they not been warned to expect the horrors of ground-shaking explosions and huge buildings tumbling down upon defenceless civilians? They began to feel that perhaps their country was going to be let off lightly, that, after all, the Germans had changed their minds about extending their territory north and west and then across the Channel.

In February 1940 the British Red Cross and Order of St John War Organisation advertised for volunteer drivers for service abroad. Winton decided to resign from the ARP and within ten days was on his way to France driving an ambulance, having passed his driving test and undergone a medical examination. He was a member of the first unit to be sent overseas, inspected at Buckingham Palace by King George VI and Queen Elizabeth prior to leaving. The volunteers received ten shillings (50p.) each week as pocket money.

On 18 March, the first unit, consisting of 25 ambulances, each with two drivers, three staff cars and two trucks, together with a police escort, set off from central London on the journey to France. In most cases, the drivers' previous experience had been a five-minute test run and the drive to Buckingham Palace! The convoy caused confusion among the early morning London traffic (such as it was in 1940).

The boat which should have been awaiting them at Newhaven had been delayed by bad weather and when they did set off the next night there were three choices of accommodation: suffocating in the hold, freezing on deck, or the comparative privacy, though equally freezing, inside the ambulances. On arrival at Dieppe the following day they journeyed in convoy to Wimereux where they found comfortable billets in two *pensions* complete with *mesdames* and staff; they were well looked after.

After setting up camp, morning and afternoon parades took up most of their days. The vehicles were new and had done very low mileage, but the drivers were instructed to clean the chromium bumpers on the ambulances (which could be seen a mile off) until they gleamed, as a hostess would shine her silver for an important dinner party.

There were occasional practice convoy runs and a little drill. The unit consisted of several elderly men, many of whom were in poor physical shape. Sport was out of the question and some organised physical exercises would have done a power of good.

Most of the volunteers did not know what to do with themselves during their free afternoons. Winton suggested first-aid classes, but received little co-operation or encouragement from the officer in command who stated the he did not believe in first aid! To be in the uniform of the Red Cross, driving ambulances with the emblem looming large, without any basic medical knowledge seemed to Winton to be madness. He was frustrated, anxious and desperate; above all, he was overwhelmed by the total incompetence and waste and could only hope that the fighting forces were better organised and the government knew what they were doing.

The officers were a motley lot, full of their own self importance; with gold braid, peeked caps and batons they became little gods. They came and went for all sorts of oblique reasons. Many were very low in intelligence; one, despite his superb knowledge of horses, was barely literate. Another turned up with his servant! Their own comfort was their main concern. It was hard to see why they were chosen and several were sent back after very few weeks. It was not surprising that morale was low and many drivers withdrew. Of the 50 who made up the unit inspected by the King and Queen in March, by September only five remained.

However, all was to change in May, by which time there were

ten British divisions deployed in the area around the border with Belgium. On 10 May 1940, at 4.30am, the German offensive began; enemy bombers flew over at no more than 300 feet, targeting the aerodrome at Le Touquet. Standing outside their barracks with overcoats over their pyjamas, the Red Cross volunteers gazed up at the planes, seeing for the first time the thick crosses on the wings and the sinister swastikas, the faces of the pilots clearly visible. As they heard the bombs falling, they threw themselves on the ground. Winton is convinced that this was the moment he experienced the greatest fear in his whole life. It had all happened without warning. There was no return of fire, not a single RAF plane left the ground – it all seemed unreal. Their immediate thoughts were 'what was happening elsewhere?'. There was no communication. Not one of their officers left his bed!

This was just the beginning. The raids continued relentlessly for ten days with little, if any, retaliation from the allies. Then began the trek of refugees. This mixed bunch of British volunteers were seeing, for the first time, the reality of war – not watching a cinema screen nor listening to a radio bulletin.

The railway line ran near to the camp and for three days, after the invasion of the Low Countries, was a hive of activity; trains passed at ten-minute intervals, day and night, carrying allied soldiers and equipment to the ever-receding front. Tanks, guns, ammunition, searchlights and every kind of military gear was transported in enormous bulk. At times the Red Cross unit felt encouraged and heartened by what appeared to them to be the strength of the allies. At other times they felt bewildered and ill-prepared for what they were facing and, with little news filtering through, they did not know what to think.

The trains continued to pass in a never-ending stream, but once Holland was occupied, they travelled in the opposite direction and with a different cargo. Now people, mostly women and children, filled the carriages, all fleeing from Belgium. Convoys were still attempting to reach the front by road – but all too late. In a matter of days, what was left of those same convoys, now manned by dejected soldiers, passed the camp, withdrawing to the coast. The unit was constantly put on alert.

The columns of fleeing people reminded Winton of scenes from countries that had been occupied by the German Army in 1938 and 1939 which had appeared in newspapers and on cinema screens of the time. Overfilled cars with mattresses tied to the roofs; weary people walking beside their vehicles, to where, they did not know; old folk, young folk, babes in arms; large showy cars, family cars, vans, lorries, motorbikes; on horseback, in farm wagons, horse-drawn carts, even steamrollers and dustcarts – anything with wheels. Then the stragglers, footsore, exhausted, bewildered, with whatever they could bring on their backs. A never-ending stream of human misery.

The members of the Red Cross unit could be no more than spectators to this tragedy. They attended to those whose feet were sore and blistered, the sprained ankles, the grazes, the cuts and bruises – there was little more they could do.

The Germans were advancing at a frightening speed, 30 or 40 miles a day, receiving little opposition and on the night of 20 May they occupied Abbeville, thus forming a trap for the allied forces, the sea being the only outlet. The confusion became more acute when some of the refugees chose to return to their homes since it appeared that the whole of Europe was soon to be overrun by the Germans. Army convoys could no longer get through. Bombers were overhead and many refugees were killed at this stage. The local village shops could not cope and food ran out quickly.

The Red Cross drivers purchased what cigarettes they could and passed them to the refugees. Some had been on the train for days aware that they were going round in circles, passing the same stations two or three times. Feeling disheartened and hopeless and no longer able to think positively, they had lost interest in where they were going.

Ironically they had named their hut 'The Retreat' and on 21 May instructions were received to evacuate Camier Camp; they joined the interminable line of assorted vehicles making their way north. The pace was slow and where the Camier road crossed the railway track they came to a halt. Here there were thousands of human bodies, interwoven with anything that could move on two, four, six or eight wheels. Seen from the air it was an unmissable target – and the Germans took advantage. Within seconds, despite the large visible red crosses on the ambulances, bombs rained down and machine guns burst their bullets out onto this mass of unarmed people. A building collapsed, blocking the road. There were surprisingly few fatalities, but the injured had to be attended to and the poorly trained Red Cross personnel did all they could. People took cover in ditches and behind trees, ready for a repeat attack and, true enough, the bombers returned for a second gunning down. Two British fighters appeared from nowhere and scared them off. This gave a moment of short-lived courage to the crowd.

The convoy arrived in Sangatte, ten kilometres west of Calais, from where two of their officers proceeded to Dunkirk for instructions; they were never seen again, having met up with the main unit in Dunkirk they departed with them for England. (One of those officers later held an important position in the Ministry of Transport!) The remaining members of the unit were left awaiting directions that never came. After 24 hours without news, two of the drivers departed for Calais to seek information, only to discover that the boat with the rest of the personnel had left; they were instructed to proceed to Dunkirk first thing the following morning, but after only 20 kilometres, were ordered to return to Calais. The following day they were told to abandon the first-aid post and, together with the wounded, the remaining members of the unit embarked for Dover where there was a wait of four hours for a tug to tow them into the harbour. Many of the wounded were in a critical condition and everyone was exhausted and bewildered.

Back in England the situation was no better. Within the unit, which was run rather like an inefficient, impecunious, low-grade boarding school, without discipline and with little respect for the officers, distrust grew among the men. Members of the armed services were given leave every three months, but the Red Cross drivers and crew were allowed one week every six months. If extra leave was requested for special reasons it would be granted, but without any fares home or maintenance allowances being paid and the small amount of money they were receiving would be stopped. Thus, those without private means or savings were deprived of any bereavement or emergency leave.

Great Britain now stood alone. Winton's recent experience and escape from France made him seriously question his pacifism. In Prague the previous year, he had seen first hand how the brutalism of the Nazi regime was perpetrated by the members of the SS; he knew that it was no myth, the ideology of Hitler and his henchmen was far-reaching and they meant business – bad business. They were now a mere 22 miles across the Channel from Dover.

* * *

Winton remained with the Red Cross for a further year and was constantly on call during the Battle of Britain; he was in Coventry after the devastation of that city in April 1941. From April until September 1942 he was in the Home Guard, but he was now anxious to be nearer the front line.

Winton had made numerous solo flights. Flying had become a passion – he loved the excitement of piloting a plane, of being alone in that vast expanse of cloud and sky watching the world of man slipping away beneath him. It seemed appropriate to enlist in the Royal Air Force, but to his disappointment his poor sight prevented him from serving as a pilot. His first posting, as a Link Trainer Instructor, teaching pilots a particular technique for night flying, was to South Cerney Aerodrome; in 1944 he was sent to La Rochelle, in western France, where he taught French pilots. He achieved the rank of Flight Lieutenant.

* * *

Towards the end of 1944 Winton was appointed second in charge of an RAF exhibition travelling to Brussels, Paris, Lyons, Oslo, Rotterdam and Prague. The exhibition travelled close on the heels of the retreating German Army and each opening took place in cities soon after their liberation. Attendances exceeded all expectations, reaching 500,000 in Brussels and 100,000 in Prague. Royalty, government officials and top brass visited the various venues. Winton kept a diary as he travelled from one war-torn town to the next.

The journey across the Belgian/Holland frontier was bleak. They arrived in Aachen where barely a house remained standing: 'Hardly anyone was to be seen in the streets and it appeared like a deserted city. Those we did see were for the most part, pushing handcarts with their belongings.' In Jülich things were worse:

> If Aachen is dead, then this place is already buried ... Saw only three people in the whole place and there can't be many walls standing higher than five feet. One has to see these places to grasp what total desctruction means. It is far worse than I ever imagined and gave me the most terrible feeling.

He wondered where the people had gone – where they were living. In Cologne, however, life was beginning anew and there were signs of new growth in the fields; coils of smoke gently rose from the chimneys of houses and farm buildings. A few of the larger factories on the outskirts of towns gave signs of resumed activity, even though the city centre was in ruins. On their entire route through Germany, from the coast to Cologne, they saw only three German vehicles: a bus, a lorry with a trailer carrying bricks and a motorbike. There were very few bicycles.

In Cologne they spent the night in a cold, damp transit camp. The vehicles had to be guarded through the night and rotas were organised. Crowds gathered wanting to buy, or more to the point, barter for, food and cigarettes in exchange for bottles of spurious brandy (probably concocted from potatoes) or small amounts of farm produce.

With his near fluent German Winton found himself communicating with the villagers who were prompted to be more truthful than they otherwise might have been. The general attitude surprised him; most considered the armistice a 'liberation' – they did not think of themselves as conquered. Winton and his colleagues were warmly welcomed and often embarrassed by the offers of food in short supply.

The autobahns, the first motorways in Europe, had been the great pride of the Nazis and, even in their present damaged state, it was a novelty to travel such distances without going through towns and villages. With just one lane open, the other being littered with debris from the destroyed bridges, travel on these roads was relatively easy going. However, they met with several diversions and saw far more of Germany than they anticipated.

In the American zone, it was neither warmer nor more comfortable, but the food was good and plentiful. Frankfurt was an unforgettable mess, hardly a building standing. Ironically the huge I.G. Farben complex appeared undamaged and the American army had commandeered various buildings for their official offices, among them the Visitors' Bureau, to which Winton had instructions to report. He did not find the Americans, in their official capacity, friendly or co-operative; the group had great difficulty in getting petrol, without which they could not continue their journey and the Americans bluntly refused to supply them with any food. The convoy was continually told that it would be easier in the next town.

Witnessing the never-ending devastation as they continued their journey affected Winton greatly – he had seen nothing comparable in England. Why, he asked himself, had it seemed necessary to so utterly wreck these towns and villages and cause such death, destruction and misery to civilians. The pattern became familiar – roads lined with rubble between empty shells of buildings, the less dangerous structures hastily improvised to shelter homeless families.

The convoy passed through several small villages that had escaped the bombs and the picture-postcard beauty of the farm buildings with their first coating of snow and the children on home-made toboggans or slides revelling in their adventures brought some relief. The laughter of the children rang out; laughter was seldom heard.

There was no obvious demarcation line between the American and Russian zones: 'No one was quite sure of the Russian sector, nor could I find out whether the Americans had just moved in or were just moving out of Pilsen and whether, if they had moved out, the Russians were now there.' Nor was anyone prepared to predict which would be the quickest route to Prague – through the Russian section from Bamberg, or from Nürnberg through the American zone – and whether refuelling would prove less or more difficult on either route. Winton decided to send part of the convoy direct to Nürnberg, whilst he set off in the Hillman via Bamberg.

Bamberg was quite lively with plenty of people going about their daily work, the city was in reasonably good shape. Winton's spirits were lifted somewhat at the sight of people seeming to have some purpose to their lives, but it was back to the depressing atmosphere of the ravaged cities when he arrived in Nürnberg – the city of his maternal antecedents.

What had been a magnificent mediaeval city was unrecognisable. Broken pieces of ancient bricks and roof tiles, of columns and sculpted façades, all jumbled together in huge piles of unsorted rubble. There was the now familiar sight of hungry people crowding round pleading, rather than begging, for even the smallest amount of food or cigarettes. Winton did not feel a conquerer, he just saw what a waste war was, what an appalling condition man had created from greed and misguided ideology.

It was impossible to find one's way about, there were no such things as road signs – the roads were unidentifiable. Winton knew the war trials were in progress, but other than a strong presence of American Military Police, there was little indication that one of the most important legal events of the twentieth century was taking place. Familiar historical figures, whose faces had constantly appeared in print and on cinema screens for the past 12 years, were incarcerated within a few hundred metres and were appearing daily in the courts. Of this, little, if anything, was discussed either by the American army of occupation, or the few Germans Winton spoke to.

It was dark when Winton's convoy got on its way. The Americans were, at this time, pulling out of Czechoslovakia. A never-ending stream of heavy traffic, with headlights glaring, was proceeding in the opposite direction. It was bitterly cold, with sporadic snow flurries, and the strain of night driving was beginning to have an effect on the drivers. Each time they made a stop to refuel, there were problems; they were rarely in possession of the necessary papers. Travel documents should have been available in Frankfurt, but there had been a slip-up. The American Army personnel, in general, were arrogant, giving the impression that the British would never have won the war without their help and there was little respect or attention given to the convoy. There was certainly no interest in their venture. It was a demeaning experience. Each time Winton purchased 50 gallons of petrol, five copies of the documents had to be sent back to London to be approved by some cabinet department. These events put everybody in bad humour.

They made their way towards the Czech border and beyond to Pilsen where they expected to hit the Russian zone within 20 miles. The snow-covered roads were dangerously icy and they moved slowly with further frustrations on the way. After 11 days they finally reached Prague.

It was after dark when they arrived in this beautiful baroque city causing a stir, bedraggled though they and their vehicles were. They booked into the Hotel Paris and were well looked after. The British Embassy was contacted and the cars were unpacked almost immediately.

The city was lively and bright at night, the people well dressed. Winton was surprised how few Russians were to be seen; the few they came across were army officers.

It is astonishing that today Winton is unable to recall his reactions on returning to Prague. His letters to his mother from this time are tedious with endless details of the setting-up of the exhibition, the important people who attended and the great success of the entire project. He makes no mention of his feelings or memories of those weeks spent in that city in 1939; weeks packed with incidents and emotions. It is hard to believe that they could have been blocked out of his memory. He was, after all, still a young man – he was 36. Did he not, for one moment, ponder on the outcome of his enormous achievement six years previously; did he not wonder what had happened to any of the 669 children? Did he not remember the tears – and the parents who were left behind? Details of the horrors of the camps were now being revealed and the unimaginable numbers of the dead beginning to haunt the world, particularly the

Jewish communities of the United States and Great Britain. It is obvious that he did not consider the role he played in saving the children to hold a higher priority than anything else he had achieved in his life. He has always said 'It was a job I had to do – like all the others.' At that moment, the exhibition held the most important place in his mind; when that was over he would be onto the next job. That is how he was.

There is just one reference to establish that his earlier visit to Prague was discussed with his superior officers. A telegram dated 22 December 1945 to the Air Ministry in Whitehall from the Air Attaché in Prague reads: 'Much regret Winton's posting. Is it possible to defer this, at least until end of run in Prague? Winton has valuable pre-war contacts which are proving of immense help ...' The Air Attaché wanted to hold on to Winton as he knew how able he was. The 'pre-war contacts' had been, in the main, non-Czechs who had to leave by the outbreak of war for their own safety, but no doubt there may have been some Czech officials Winton was able to look up and who were helpful. Prague was a very different place from that with which he had become familiar in 1939. He stayed with the Exhibition until it closed early in 1946.

His old friend Martin Blake, the catalyst in the whole drama of the *kindertransports,* was in Prague at the time with his wife, Barbara. He was still working for the British Council. Winton and he had dinner together several times during his stay there but cannot recall any details of their conversations; surely the subject of the saving of the children would have come up?

Back in London, the war over, it was a time of hope and looking forward. He must now give thought to how he was to spend the rest of his life.

LOOKING FORWARD: 1946–48

After demobilisation from the Royal Air Force in 1946 Winton, having witnessed the misery and trauma of incarceration and displacement and aware of the thousands of persons still in camps all over Europe with nowhere to go, wished to involve himself in the task of rehabilitation and resettlement.

At the Evian Conference in 1938, the Intergovernmental Committee for Refugees was established, replacing the League of Nations Refugee Office, with its headquarters in London. It seemed an appropriate organisation for the work Winton had in mind and he was accepted as a member of the committee, his fluent German possibly making him an attractive applicant. The merging of the London office with the International Refugee Organisation in 1947 found Winton relocated to Geneva.

He took up his appointment as assistant to Abba Schwartz, Reparations Director of the Preparatory Commission of the International Refugee Organisation (PCIRO), believing that his responsibilities would be concerned with the well-being of displaced persons and helping to improve the conditions in which they were being held. Indeed, his first duties were just that.

The atmosphere in Geneva was certainly very different from the austere situation left behind in London. Winton could not have envisaged the life of luxury which was to be his in Switzerland; the clinically clean, modern offices, the up-to-date typewriters and copying machines, the teleprinters were a novelty and fascinated him. It was altogether another world – a cocooned, protected, almost sterile atmosphere with copious committees and never-ending meetings. A salary triple the amount he had received in London and no tax to pay was all very pleasant, but that was not what he had in mind when he was attracted to the organisation. It was not long, however, before he was able to get down to the real work which took him away from the well-ordered routine of Geneva.

His first assignment took him to Frankfurt. Together with Father Killion, the IRO representative from the Vatican, they had instructions to arrange for approximately 100 families to leave the displacement camp and begin a new life elsewhere. Every step taken presented difficulties, creating a pattern for all the transactions during the following months. The town was still in ruins with the rubble just as he had seen it lying around in 1945 on his journey to Prague with the RAF exhibition. At that time a dazed population had neither the energy nor the inclination to bar his way. Then, only the frontiers had been guarded; now, the Americans inspected identification papers four times on the stretch between Baden-Baden and Frankfurt, each time under cover of machine guns.

Neither of them had any money; the only legal tender was American 'scrip'. Having arrived on a Saturday, the US Exchange was closed; the Airways Office was open but unable or unwilling to help; and the British, who were even less interested in their plight, suggested the American Express who were sorry, but they had strict instructions only to accept travellers' cheques and not dollar notes. 'Stop a GI', they suggested, 'he will help you.'

Since American Army personnel were not allowed to possess dollar bills this was an official invitation to step into the black market. They found an army sergeant who said he was a bit tight, but hastened to add that he did have $1,600 in scrip in his pocket and was on his way to buy a Chevrolet! He helped out with $20. In general, the American GIs Winton saw around were newly conscripted youngsters who had not seen the real desecration of Germany, nor had they fought in the battles preceding the armistice. War, to them, was how to make easy money, abuse the former enemy, stand superior and enjoy the good-time girls of whom there were plenty. None of this was discouraged by their officers. Goods could be purchased in the PX stores, as much or as many as they could buy. The Germans would go to great lengths to obtain such commodities. These boys were 10 or 12 years old when the war began and were totally ignorant of the causes that brought it about – at times Winton wondered if they had ever heard of Hitler.

Winton had to get to Berlin with some urgency. Travel documents had to be purchased at the I.G. Farben building, remarkably untouched by the bombing, where inside, all was chaos. After one hour in the wrong office he eventually got hold of the necessary papers in a second office, but required an additional document from a third office which was, by this time, closed. He was already behind schedule, but had to remain in Frankfurt over a US holiday.

Frustrated, but determined to see the job through, he used

any spare moment to see for himself what was going on in this devastated city. In the centre of Frankfurt he met a man who told him he was 63 and had been called up only three years previously. He offered to show him the ruins of the old town.

People were climbing over the rubble to get to the cellars they had made their homes. The shells of huge buildings towered above, looking decidedly unsafe; the Paulskirche, the Dome, the Römer. Only the Paulskirche showed signs of restoration. The Römer had been a magnificent Romanesque church in which former kings had been crowned. In the centre of the square stood a fountain, the Gerechtigkeitsbrunnen (The Fountain of Justice) in which a young girl holds a fragile pair of scales – amazingly undamaged in the midst of such destruction. In the shell of what was the town's cathedral, the Dome, a small chapel had been repaired just sufficiently to enable services to be held – a sanctuary in an arid wilderness.

Winton returned to the oasis which was the Carlton Hotel where he had an excellent dinner for 60 cents, but felt uncomfortable with his position of privilege. Feeling restless and with a degree of curiosity, he took another walk, this time wandering towards the station where he came across a large crowd, mostly young males, shabby and unkempt. Not being in any uniform, he was taken for a German civilian and was soon either offered or requested anything from bread and meat coupons to chocolate and cigarettes by young lads, many of whom were disabled. Scrip dollars and marks were changing hands. People were hungry and the farmers would only supply food on a barter basis. The crowd would disperse if a policeman was in sight, only to meet again and start transactions within a few minutes. There was no law.

Winton was told of a GI who had purchased a painting by Van Dyck from a former antique dealer for 2,000,000 marks he had made from the sale of cigarettes! He wondered where that painting had ended up.

In the midst of this confused and disorderly atmosphere Winton had a job to do and it was essential to place himself apart from the hopelessness and misery that existed wherever he looked. He did not find it easy.

* * *

Some months later Winton was entrusted with a task, the background to which he would never have believed possible. He was given the job of organising the sale of Nazi booty found in the American zone of occupation. Who could be prepared for such work? Stories of stolen art and jewellery that had seeped out of the occupied zones of Germany were in the main disbelieved. There was no kind of training or experience that could qualify one for such a task – it was one without precedent – a task that was to take him to Berlin, Bremerhaven, Hamburg, Bremen; to Zurich, Berne, Basel and Paris; to Washington, New York and Halifax in Nova Scotia; even to Manchester.

Jewellery, china, silver, rugs and other valuables had been found close to a liberated concentration camp. Dumped in French powder kegs, German ammunition boxes and other salvaged military containers, the booty was subsequently stored in air-raid shelters. The material had originally been sorted by 'Jew workers' in the camps; men who were saved, most often temporarily, from the gas chambers because of their youth, strength and fitness.

In accordance with the Five Power Agreement of 14 June 1946 (the governments of the United States of America, the United Kingdom, France, Czechoslovakia and Yugoslavia), a plan was to be put in motion 'to aid in the rehabilitation and resettlement of non-repatriable victims of German Action'.

Twenty-five million dollars (think of that sum in today's terms!) from Nazi assets in neutral countries (mainly Switzerland) would be advanced 'plus an indeterminate amount of heirless funds in banks throughout the world also designated for reparations to Nazi victims to be administered by the PCIRO'. The money was to be used 'not for the compensation of individual victims, but for the rehabilitation and resettlement of persons in eligible classes and the expenditures on rehabilitation shall be considered as essential preparatory outlays to resettlement'. It was agreed that 'since all available statistics indicate beyond any reasonable doubt that the overwhelming majority of eligible persons are Jewish', 90 per cent of the $25,000,000 already mentioned and the same percentage of the proceeds of non-monetary gold, plus 9 per cent of the heirless funds, should be distributed to Jewish victims. The remainder was to be administered by the Intergovernment Committee on Refugees for the rehabilitation of the relatively small numbers of non-Jewish victims of Nazi action.

Winton was to be responsible for supervising the grisly work of appraising, packing and ultimately transforming the metals contained in these hoards of personal belongings into anonymous and impersonal gold bars. Two diamond experts were flown in from the United States to advise on the quality and value of the gems.

It was not an easy time for Winton:

> The job expected of me during my time with the IRO was one that will stay in my memory forever. It lies in a corner of my mind that never ceases to be overwhelmed by the very scale of the incubus of the Holocaust. There I was in Germany and around me were those very people who, but three years before, had been witness to, and many involved in, the enforcement of such bestial horror, whatever else they might now suggest.

In addition to the loot found by the American Army, a large amount of various currencies was discovered in the Reichsbank. Inspecting these scores of thousands of notes took hours and hours; each note had to be carefully examined and then checked to see whether or not it was current legal tender. American Express arranged for a 15-ton truck to transport the 24 crates (only four of which contained currency of any value) to Julius Baer and Company, merchant bankers in Zurich. Winton accompanied the freight. At the border, Swiss customs let the currency through with little comment, but demanded a considerable duty on the 20 crates of 'waste paper'!

At this time the first consignment of 844 cases, valued at approximately $1,000,000, was ready for shipment: 334 cases of silver bowls, candlesticks and plate; 198 cases of table silver; 132

cases of rugs; 130 cases of china; 34 cases of watches, clocks, jewels and cigarette cases; 16 cases of valuable postage stamps. These were to be sold in the United States by a Merchandising Advisory Committee of the PCIRO. Diamonds valued at $500,000 had previously been flown to the United States and the gold and silver bullion obtained from the smelting of 'non-monetary gold' was being prepared for sale.

Winton recalls one bizarre load amongst this cargo. Once the cases of the myriad watches had been removed, the sorters were left with the watch workings and, as they were under strict orders not to allow any material, of however little value, to remain on German soil, they were faced with the problem of disposal. A decision was taken to crate up these clock and watch innards, load them onto the boat, and throw them overboard in mid-ocean. At times, whilst handling this material, an alarm would be heard from within a crate. An eerie sound – whoever had set that alarm would never awaken.

Winton travelled with the cargo from Geneva to Bremerhaven. Once there, the seventeen coaches, split into two sections, were shunted onto a peninsular at Columbus Quay. Each coach had been sealed in Salzburg and again in Frankfurt and these had to be inspected by Winton and a Captain Wikle, Freight and Movements Officer. Further seals were then affixed and a 24-hour armed guard took over with orders to shoot any unauthorised person approaching the train. The coaches were floodlit all night with an electrician on permanent duty in case of a power failure. Armoured cars were in position, one at each end of the train.

The cargo, with its protectors, set sail for Halifax, Nova Scotia, on board S.S. *General Sturgis* on 1 December 1947; the final destination was to be New York. The ship was one of three operated specially by the United States War Department for the PCIRO travelling across the Atlantic carrying groups of refugees to be resettled in one of the countries with which the PCIRO had a resettlement agreement. On this particular journey, the ship's sixth trip as a refugee transport, there were 856 displaced persons on board on their way to a new life in Canada, where most of them had close relatives. They would find work as lumbermen in forests, as miners, or as garment-makers. Winton was impressed with their enthusiasm for life and their eagerness to assist in the countless jobs that needed doing during the journey:

> I was able to detach myself from my responsibility for the gruesome cargo in the hold of the ship and although the crossing was very rough at times, with passengers disappearing to their cabins for hours, even days, at a time, it was all very social. There were parties and I was invited to join in games of bridge and poker; I even won 25 cents! Two US Army officers, both Lieutenant Colonels, who had been assigned to me to assist with security, were good company. We sailed through the Gulf Stream where the cloudless sky allowed a brief, but welcome, warmth from a winter sun. Seagulls and a porpoise leaping out of the water were the only signs of life. Such serenity produced an amazing feeling of apartness – we all felt a long way from the misery of Europe.

Most of the boats sailed directly to Halifax and it was costly to arrange for them to dock and off-load in New York, but an office had been offered to them in Manhattan with secretarial help supplied by the IRO.

Once the *Sturgis* arrived in New York, unloading took the good part of two days. The crates were then stored in Staten Island to await customs clearance; in order to prepare the material for sale, the contents had to be sorted and reclassified. It was proposed at one point that a 'gigantic bazaar' should be held in Grand Central Palace or in one of the large armouries in New York – hardly an appropriate setting for this particular cargo.

* * *

Back in Germany, Winton was assigned the job of organising the smelting and refining of the precious metals contained in items forcibly abandoned by victims before entering the gas chambers. Jewellery, spectacle frames, false teeth and cigarette cases were amongst the limited possessions victims had been permitted to keep with them. Gold fillings were extracted and rings removed from the corpses before cremation.

Take a handful of gold fillings (if you are unfortunate enough to have such things) and drop them one by one onto your kitchen scales; the scales would not begin to register until there were four, maybe five. Thousands of kilograms of gold were produced from this grisly booty. There you have some idea of the scale of this mighty operation.

Winton often wondered how much was known to the wider public of the work with which he was involved. Occasionally they would have a visitor. Eleanor Roosevelt, a good friend of Schwartz, came to see what they were doing. Yehudi Menuhin, the violinist, who was much affected by what he had seen when playing for the survivors of the death camps, visited the Deutsche Bank in Berlin. He watched Winton's colleagues inspecting and sorting the treasures, the tiaras that had been worn at grand balls, necklaces, earrings, pearls, diamonds, sapphires. He was unable to utter a word.

Thirty-nine cases of gold scrap, weighed on bathroom scales at the Reichsbank, arrived at Degussa (Deutsche Gold und Silber Schiedungs Anstalt) for the smelting operation. Degussa, the largest company in Germany dealing in metals, was familiar with such work; the company had melted down huge quantities of metals for the Nazis (it will probably never be known exactly how much), but this was to be the first assignment since the end of the war. Boxes were kept sealed at the bank, with Winton the only person authorised to open them; only sufficient material for two days work was to be extracted at a time. The first job was the weighing of the gold scrap into ten kilogram lots, ready for smelting.

The smelting process produced the finest quality gold bars, other less precious metals having already been extracted. These bars were now ready for sale. It was important to keep abreast of market prices on the bullion exchange. Winton was in constant touch with banks in the UK and Switzerland. His experience and the contacts made during his city career in the 1920s proved helpful when dealing with merchant banks. At this time, January 1948, prices for silver were more favourable in

London.

One hundred and thirty crates of 'hollow' silver were sold at 45d. (19p.) per ounce. Samuel Montagu, bullion dealers, were responsible for the sale of the gold, which brought $35 an ounce, and offered their services without charge, thus saving the PCIRO considerable expenses.

In February 1948, 650 kilograms of gold and 150 kilograms of silver were ready to be transported to London. The material was to be carried on a regular British European Airways flight from Frankfurt.

Twenty boxes, their contents valued at $750,000 were taken from the vaults at the Reichsbank in Frankfurt watched by an official from the bank and an Army officer. The Reichsbank was particularly uncooperative, constantly putting obstacles in their way and arguing over trivial matters.

A delay in the departure of the plane would prove disastrous. Under an escort of five Military Police they journeyed to the airport. Winton was in the van with the bullion, a jeep following close behind, its red lights flashing, its siren blaring. They sped along the near-deserted roads, scattering pedestrians in their wake; any vehicle in sight was ordered to slow down and pull in to the side of the road by the MP Sergeant sitting beside the driver.

Winton describes the drama:

> We arrived at the airport pleased to find the plane scheduled to leave on time, but there followed a period of uneasiness and uncanny silence. It was then announced that all flights were cancelled! The Reichsbank had washed their hands of the whole procedure once the documents were signed; I was on my own. I had to make the decision to load the boxes into the wire enclosure at the airport, ask for the airport police to stand guard and stay locked in with the 'freight' for the night, but the escort of Military Police were anxious to be on their way and the airport refused to provide extra guards. After numerous telephone calls it was decided to reload the boxes back into the van, drive back into the city and deposit them in the main hall of the bank

where I would stay with them for the night. The bank had day and night guards. The reloading took place and the van sped back to town where unloading began again, only to be told that Lietutenant Colonel Emigh, of the Provost Marshall's Department, US Military Headquarters, had now been alerted and had given instructions to bring the cargo round to his flat offering me a bed for the night where I could sleep surrounded by the boxes. Two MPs would be on duty outside my door all night. For the third time, the van was loaded and we dashed through the town to the flat where I slept, my cargo beside me, and did not even wake for the 'changing of the guard'. My escort returned at 8.30 the next morning and ten minutes later we set off for the airport. We loaded the cargo onto the plane and took off, arriving at Northolt at lunchtime. Formalities on the British side of the channel were minimal!

Winton does not believe that this series of delays happened by chance:

The authorities were highly suspicious of me, an English civilian, in charge of a large load of gold bars attempting to leave the American occupied zone. My credentials must have been checked pretty thoroughly. Communication in those days was not that easy – no fax, no e-mail.

* * *

Profit from the sale of the precious metals of $728,000 was distributed by PCIRO to voluntary agencies according to the Paris Agreement. Arrangements were made for a further 8,000 kilograms of silver scrap to be sent from Salzburg to the Sheffield Smelting Company for smelting and sale which subsequently brought in another $300,000.

In March 1948, 6,000 kilograms of silver were transported from Frankfurt to Tangiers and the final 200 kilograms arrived in London by air.

Winton wrote to Dave Rolbein at Head Office, on 13 February 1948: 'The gold has been delivered and $700,000 is being paid to us today on account.' The culmination of a business transaction?

I look at those words today and do not feel as I did then. At the time I suppose it did resemble a business transaction – I had the goods, I arranged for their transport and they were paid for – what else could you call it? Today I think not only of all those innocent lives, senselessly and horrifically cut off, most of them in their prime, but of the depraved minds obsessed with the material gains to be obtained from pitiable items so small and so personal. A million wedding rings alone. At the time it was a job I had to do and I suppose I had a sense of pride and achievement in having succeeded in my mission.

* * *

A cable received on 20 March 1948 from Abba Schwarz read:

THANKS. COMPLETION FRANKFURT OPERATION.

This story concerns a minute fraction of the loot and the operation itself received a minimum of publicity at the time. There has always been a great deal of speculation as to what happened to the riches accumulated by the Nazis. For 50 years there was an uncanny silence on the subject. Only since 1997, when evidence of a cover-up by the Swiss banks on the vexed question of money and valuables deposited by Holocaust victims and the difficulties entailed in proving possession by their families, has there been extensive world-wide media coverage.

A CHANGE OF DIRECTION: 1948 AND AFTER

Winton's lifestyle changed considerably after the excitement of his work for the IRO. His day-to-day routine was calmer; he had time to participate in social engagements. One could say that he had been fortunate in having more than his fair share of drama in his working life, certainly in the first 40 years, but his personal life was comfortable and steady, and had continued on an even keel. He is taciturn on the subject of relationships, but he was, and is today, good company and quite gregarious. He had always been close to his family, particularly his mother, who had lived on her own from 1934 until her death in 1979.

In 1948, Winton joined the International Bank in Paris. At that time loans were being made to the various European countries struggling with their economies after the effects of six years of war, in an effort to get them back on their feet. The administration was not efficient and the conditions of many of the promised loans were not met. Winton was allotted the near impossible task of ensuring that the money received was not used for military purposes; the Americans insisted on sending over their own personnel rather than employ Europeans whom they considered untrained in modern banking methods; the French, understandably, believed their jobs to be in jeopardy and did their best to resist the order. Eventually the Paris branch was closed.

Grete Gjelstrup, a 29-year-old Danish girl, was secretary to the European Director of the Bank when Winton and she met in Paris early in 1948. She fell madly in love with the suave Englishman and was so confident of her feelings that when Winton asked her to marry him she said, without hesitation, 'Yes, please!'. Their courtship was brief and they married in Vejle, Denmark, in October of that year. It was a formal wedding in evening dress. The organist, with respect for the English guests, without warning played the British National Anthem during a quiet moment in the church service, at which point the English visitors, lead by Stanley Murdoch who was best man, stood to attention, thus delaying the proceedings and causing great mirth amongst the rest of the congregation.

The newlyweds found an apartment in Passy, near the centre of the city, not far from the river, and entertained frequently; it was a very happy time, free of cares. Their guests were an interesting mixture, few of whom were natives of Paris; they included the Czech conductor, Rafael Kubelik, Jean Weidner, who had been head of the Dutch resistance in France, and

Martin and Barbara Blake who were to make irregular appearances throughout Winton's life. Frederick Handl, his mother's old friend, also visited.

There was no oven; they improvised with an open fire and a grid where they cooked duck; ice was hauled up from the courtyard to the bathroom window and kept in the bidet! Grete was an excellent cook, as I was later to find out; at some point she took a cordon bleu cookery course.

They purchased a little Citroën, a *deux chevaux*, and toured around northern France, visiting chateaux and walking. Winton played in various fencing matches. He was offered an attractive job in Washington, DC, but decided against it as he and Grete wanted time to think about where they should settle down and raise a family.

Their dollar salaries during the past few years had been quite considerable (and seemed to them quite absurd). It would not have been prudent to change the dollars into sterling; they decided to have a last fling and set sail for the United States on board the *Ile de France* with plans to tour the country for three months and enjoy themselves.

The crossing itself was exciting. Winton's cousin was on the same boat, travelling first class, and they were often invited to dine with him, where they saw Errol Flynn 'propping up the bar' each evening.

At that time, there were few European tourists visiting the States. As foreigners, Nicky and Grete were a novelty, particularly in small towns where it was thought that anyone coming to America must be considering emigration. They were considered crazy to return to the hardships of England. They travelled throughout the States in their rented car, with a brief trip over the border to Canada. In Washington, they visited the World Bank and spent time with Abba Schwartz with whom Winton had worked in Geneva. They positively marvelled at the sights and were painfully aware of the lack of understanding of, or even interest in, the tragedy of Europe, particularly outside the big towns. They saw the Blue Ridge Mountains, New Orleans, the Gulf of Mexico and Florida, which was then very rural with few tourists to be seen; they stayed with friends in

Ottawa where they tapped maple syrup in the snow and finally sailed home in a happy state of mind, on a converted troop ship.

* * *

On their return to England they could no longer delay the decision making. They were slightly overwhelmed by the choices open to them – the possibilities of making their home in America, Denmark or England. America had been a great experience; after austere Europe, with its huge post-war problems, everything seemed luxurious and the people friendly, welcoming and apparently free of cares. On their extensive travels throughout the States they had seen diverse lifestyles, some of them attractive and tempting; job opportunities were there for the taking, but they thought of themselves essentially as Europeans and never seriously considered making their life there. They chose to settle in England – a decision they never regretted. Winton felt very English and was deeply attached to the country of his birth.

Equally important was the question of earning a living. One thing was for sure – he was not returning to the Stock Exchange. They moved in with his sister who was living in Belsize Park, North London, whilst they made up their minds where to start house hunting. After the comparative excitement and mobility of all his previous work experiences everything seemed tame. When his mother mentioned that she had met someone at her bridge club who was looking for a partner to develop a factory, which he had just taken over in Maidenhead, making ice lollipops, Winton, with great apprehension, decided to take up the offer. The two partners developed the business until, some years later, it was bought out by the Lyons group. Working for a large organisation was not one little bit to Winton's liking and after a few miserable years he left. His next business move was to an engineering firm, but he soon came to the conclusion that the world of business was not for him.

A house was purchased in Maidenhead in 1950 where their three children were born. Their first child, Nicholas, in 1952 and a daughter, Barbara, in 1953.

In 1956, Robin was born. He seemed a bonny enough baby at birth, but there were soon signs that all was not well. In the maternity home after the delivery, the doctor had pronounced the baby fit, but at the post-natal check-up a nurse suggested they have a chat with their general practitioner who asked them quite directly: 'Has no one told you that Robin is a Mongol?'[2] By this time Robin was six months old. The shock to the family was profound; from that moment their lifestyle was transformed.

Winton had got into the habit of making notes of important events and experiences in his life. At that time he wrote:

> ... up 'til then, we could still dream that all would be well, it wasn't true, it could be cured, we could live with Alice in Wonderland and make ourselves believe anything – anything except the truth. All that was past – the present was fact and had to be faced.

Grete and Nicholas had been spared any previous experience of mental handicap, but now unfortunately found themselves completely without professional advice. There was little assistance or sympathy to be had from the medical profession; the local authority did not want to be involved; their family doctor had misinformed them; they took it upon themselves to investigate the condition. A great deal of their misery could have been avoided had there been better help available.

They learnt that there would be good chances to reach their child's mind on a one-to-one basis within the family unit; that these children react to love and attention – whatever their general physical or mental potential; that such potential would be certain to be greatly increased by the care given at home in a loving environment as against the less individual attention which would be provided in an institution.

They agonised over what was best, not only for Robin, but for their other two children, who might grow to resent the extra attention given to their brother and wish he had been sent away. Later, they asked themselves, would Nicholas and Barbara feel they could not bring friends home.

Advice was offered by friends and relatives in all kindness, but the parents knew that only they could make the big decision to have Robin at home or send him away.

Their doctor recommended that he be sent away, almost without discussion, advising them that the extra work would disrupt the family life with possible serious results in relationships, particularly when the children were older.

Knowing how family orientated the Wintons were, their friends advised them differently. They admitted to certain risks, but considered a far greater risk would be the guilt the parents would experience if Robin were to be sent away to an institution. It was known that children with this condition were most loving and would, in all probability, give the family great happiness, despite the extra attention needed to care for them. 'We kept Robin at home and have never for one moment regretted this decision.'

Robin's routine during the first year was little different from that of any other child. He gave little trouble at night and his parents soon became adjusted to the responsibility they had undertaken. An attractive, happy and much loved little boy, with a great sense of humour, his well-being became the central consideration of any family arrangement. Although he was never able to walk or speak and required help with feeding, he was a wonderful influence on the family's life – he laughed so much. As he grew older, the work involved in caring for their son was immense, particularly as he was also afflicted with a heart condition.

Winton's mother had great difficulty in coming to terms with the fact that she had a mentally handicapped grandson. 'Why should this happen to us?', she would constantly ask. When she visited the family, she did not know how to behave and could not handle Robin as the immediate family had all learnt to do.

His happiness in the smallest of things – just the catching of a ball thrown to him by his siblings – brought the family close. 'He gave us an understanding, not only of ourselves, but of others. We learnt a lot from him during his short life.' He died, aged seven, in 1962.

The only communication from the medical officer was received three months after Robin's death, saying that he had

1. Nicholaus Wertheim, Winton's paternal grandfather.

2. Rudolf Wertheim, Winton's father, c.1900.

3. In the garden at Cleve Road; Winton with his maternal grandmother, Aunt Ida, Uncle Emil and sister, Lottie, c.1910.

4. Rudolf Wertheim in British Army uniform, c.1916.

5. Watch innards and other items of no value being thrown overboard. Winton is on the right, wearing glasses.

6. Watch innards having been removed.

7. Winton and his mother, Barbara, 1948.

8. Winton fencing, c.1931. This was his favourite sport, in which he excelled.

9. Winton's mother working in the London office, c.1939.

10. Winton and co-drivers, during his time with the ambulance service in France, 1940.

11. Winton with his brother and sister in Willow Road, Hampstead, c.1942.

12. Grete and Nicky Winton on their wedding day, October 1948.

13. Grete, Nicky, Nicky's sister and brother and Grete's sister, Kirsten, 1948.

14. The famous scrapbook, discovered in Winton's attic in 1988, detailing events in 1938–39.

REPORT ON THE PROBLEM OF REFUGEE CHILDREN IN CZECHO-SLOVAKIA .

It is not possible at the moment to give exact figures of the number of children in Czecho-Slovakia who must be evacuated. This is due to the fact that many middle-class families, when they were forced to leave their homes, first of all went to friends. At that time they thought that provision would be made for them within a very short time. Now, however, that four months have elapsed, these friends are unable to offer hospitality any longer, with the result that continually more and more families are officially registering themselves as refugees. A conservative estimate of the number of children who can leave Czecho-Slovakia at once is 2,000. These are roughly 85% Jewish and 15% Christian. They are very largely from the middle-class and professional people, most of the fathers having been before shop-keepers, journalists, doctors, solicitors, and so on. About 25% are of working-class families.

The position of all these refugees is desperate, for the following reasons :

1. To a great extent the parents were politically active in that part of Czecho-Slovakia which has been taken over by Germany, and therefore stand under the daily fear and often threat of being returned to Germany.

2. The refugees leaving the occupied areas were not able to do so in any orderly manner: that is to say, to a very large extent they had to leave their homes with only a few hours notice, and therefore could only take with them those things which they were able to carry. Unlike, therefore, a great number of German and Austrian refugees, these people have the added disadvantage of being without any of their former possessions, that is to say, clothing and home.

3. Many of them believed in the original idea of the Munich Agreement, which was to the effect that there would be a plebiscite in many districts. They made their plans accordingly. Only at the very last moment were they told that such a plebiscite would not take place, and in many instances of this kind whole families had to leave their homes at night, and walk over the frontier with nothing more than what they had on, any possessions which they were carrying with them being confiscated. *Jews.*

4. *German and Austrian*
5. *Slovakia too* On arrival in the present Czecho-Slovakia, those families who had no friends were herded together and put into camps, in which the conditions are so generally known that their misery and the moral degradation under which they live in them need not be further stressed here.

Nicholas Winton.

15. February 1939 report on the problem of refugee children in Czecho-slovakia, signed by Winton.

BRITISH COMMITTEE FOR REFUGEES FROM CZECHOSLOVAKIA
CHILDREN'S SECTION
——————

Telephone: MUSeum 2900 Ext. 217

BLOOMSBURY HOUSE
Room 217,
BLOOMSBURY STREET
LONDON, W.C. 1.

Dear Sir (or Madam),

It is not generally known that a Committee dealing entirely with Refugee Children from Czechoslovakia is in existence. The purpose of this letter is therefore to state shortly how we work and what assistance we require.

Up to the end of January last (that is 4 months after Munich) there was no organisation in London dealing with the children from Czecho-slovakia. This Section of the Czech Committee was then started. From the beginning we worked under very great handicaps. The system of bringing children over in large numbers and putting them in camps had been dropped. Committees all over England had originally been formed to deal with Refugees from Germany and there was considerable haggling as to whether Czechs should be included within the Committees' scope of activity. Now this has changed and Bohemia at any rate, being a Protectorate, is considered part of Germany.

All this has resulted in the fact that up to now very little indeed has been done for the children in Czechoslovakia. A great number are German, Austrian or Sudetengerman, and have had to move more than once since they became wanderers. Their condition is appalling. Memories are short, and people are inclined to forget the misery which was caused when, for example, the plebiscite was cancelled in Sudetenland. Whole families had to leave with a few hours' notice. Their condition at the time was serious - it is now quite desperate. This poor country, which 6 months ago was the Saviour of the Peace of the World, is now almost forgotten.

Something must be done quickly to help at least the most urgent cases. Some children must be got out without delay.

At the most, only 200 children have so far left Czechoslovakia. This is a frightful position. Guarantors are available, as is evident from the number of children being brought out of Germany. Some of these guarantees must be used for our children, and I appeal most sincerely to your committee to aid us.

I have in the office case papers with photos of 5,000 children. Our office in Prague has investigated the cases and has selected from these 5,000 a list of 250 really desperately urgent cases. Will you please help us to place these children ?

The conditions are the same as those in force for bringing children from Germany. Our office in Prague is working well and we can bring any child to this country within 3 weeks of it being guaranteed.

We will be only too pleased to give you any information you may require BY RETURN.

Hoping that you will see your way to help us,

I am,

Yours faithfully,

16. Circular letter, June 1939. This was sent to other committees for refugees.

heard that they had a mentally handicapped child and could he help in any way!

Memories of Robin, although not without pain, are warm and dear to his parents; this happy child whose short life gave his immediate family remarkable pleasure, and whose death left a legacy of love without conditions or reward, later prompted Winton to devote his retirement to charitable work, particularly for MENCAP. He served as chairman to the local society and is still on the National Committee; he also lectured on the subject and the work of the society at meetings attended by families of mentally handicapped children. There are many misunderstandings concerning the difference between the mentally ill and the mentally handicapped, the latter being incurable. The quality of life for the mentally handicapped can be greatly improved by the training available today, but in the 1950s it was up to the family and that was not easy.

In the meantime the Wintons had purchased a plot of land, part of a large estate near Maidenhead and, in 1958, built the house in which he still lives.

As a member of the local Rotary Club Winton met many people who became good friends. Thus began the charity work which continues to this day. They organised fund-raising events, took elderly people out for drives, supported an eye hospital for children in India, transported the blind to their clubs and parties, and undertook dozens of other charitable duties.

At the Rotary Club Winton heard of the Abbeyfield Society, a housing association providing care and companionship for the frail and lonely elderly. There are approximately 600 branches and 1,000 homes throughout the country. Winton got together with a group of local people and raised sufficient funds to build a home in Windsor, now named Winton House, where there are 30 residents, each with their own room and bath. He remains president of the local branch.

Grete founded a movement for European Friendship in Maidenhead, with corresponding branches in the twin towns of St Cloud, France, Courtrai, Belgium, Frascati, Italy and Bad Godesberg, Germany. She was president for 15 years and the organisation continues to flourish. Each group has 40 or 50 members and they meet together every year.

Since leaving the city behind him and the pleasurable pursuits of fencing and flying, Winton has devoted his life to caring causes. He decided to retire in 1967, when only 58; since then he has continued his work with Abbeyfield and MENCAP on a voluntary basis. In 1983 he was awarded the MBE for services to the community.

* * *

Grete and Nicholas thus kept busy with their joint and individual interests and hobbies. The garden, particularly the vegetable plot, took up a lot of their time, but was always a labour of love. Both their children married and their two grandchildren gave them immense pleasure. Winton's love of music, particularly opera, was ever present and in retirement he had more time, not only to listen at home, but to attend operas in London; latterly he became a Friend of the English National Opera and until very recently would attend dress rehearsals, usually taking place in the mornings. Ever caring, he would drive up to central London, taking with him a severely disabled friend who shared his love of music.

The Wintons enjoyed travelling once or twice a year, most often to Europe, making a point of visiting the towns twinned to their own. In later years they saw the wonders of Egypt on a trip down the Nile and, a year or two before Grete's death, spent a few weeks in Tunisia. They felt their life to be exceedingly pleasant; they saw that their demands were always within their reach.

Had Winton not gone up to the attic one day and come across a pile of papers in a battered old case, he has no reason to believe that life would not have continued in similar vein until today.

But that was not to be.

NOTES

1. Margot Heinemann (1913–92), writer and academic. Daughter of German-Jewish banker, Max Heinemann and his wife Selma. Of a similar background to Winton, her parents came to the UK at the turn of the century and settled in Hampstead. After Roedean and Cambridge, she devoted her life to Communism and was the lover of the poet John Cornford (who was killed in the Spanish Civil War) and, later, companion to the physicist, J.D. Bernal.
2. An unkind and racial reference to the condition now known as Down's syndrome.

PART TWO

by Vera Gissing

2 *The Rescue Mission*

They say that life is a lottery, a game of chance. To this day I marvel that I have been spared, that I have lived to enjoy the bonus of 60 happy years, that I escaped with my sister the fate which Hitler had mapped out so meticulously for the Jewish race, that I did not perish in the Holocaust as did the rest of my family and millions of others.

If, as war clouds were gathering, my parents had lacked the courage and strength to send us, their only children, to unknown people in a foreign country, if British families had not been found to take us in, all the hopes, efforts and willingness to help would have been fruitless – had it not been for Nicholas Winton.

It is thanks to him that I am now sitting in my garden watching my grandchildren playing, listening to their laughter and to my daughter's voice calling us in for tea. Such an everyday family scene, yet one that I can never take for granted. Without Winton's help, there would have been no children or grandchildren and I would not be writing these chapters to which he refers, rather modestly, as 'a small part of my life; just something I had to do, just another job ...'.

What an understatement! The 'job' may have covered only a few brief months of his life, but it had been by far his most important job, his most remarkable achievement, the magnitude of which he only recently began to realise.

When, shortly before Christmas 1938, this 29-year-old man

was busy packing for his skiing holiday in Switzerland, he certainly could not have imagined that he would, instead, be on his way to Prague to embark on a life-saving mission, that he would take on the mammoth task of organising the mass evacuation of endangered children from Czechoslovakia. Although he was helped by other concerned individuals, it was mainly thanks to his foresight, organising ability, dedication and, more than anything, his compassion and determination to help those in need and danger that eight transports left Prague for Britain during the uneasy months prior to the outbreak of World War II, bringing 669, mainly Jewish children, to safety. Without his swift and timely intervention, the trains we boarded would not have taken us to a safe haven in Britain, but to a concentration camp and an almost certain death.

All it took was an unexpected telephone call, an impulsive change of plans and events were set in motion which had the most profound effect on Winton's life and changed the destinies of many others.

As one of those who came to Britain as a child on a transport from Prague, I often wondered over the years who was the key figure in our rescue. I was completely unaware of Winton's existence and the vital role he had played. When, in 1987, I was completing my autobiography *Pearls of Childhood* (Robson Books, 1988), I tried my utmost to find out, but, no matter where I turned or whom I approached, I drew a blank. Even among my many friends who also came on the Prague transports and spent several years with me at the Czechoslovak wartime school in Wales, there was not a single person who was any the wiser. Sadly and reluctantly I gave up the quest. But fate intervened. My lucky number was about to come up, yet again!

At that particular time, Winton was busy clearing out his attic. His aunt had died recently and he had the unenviable task of sorting out her papers. 'They were in an awful state', he said, 'I wouldn't wish such a job on anyone, least of all on my wife and my children.' Thus he decided it was high time to put his own papers in order and discard what he could.

Up in the attic Winton, then almost in his eightieth year, rummaged through boxes and suitcases which held articles, documents, letters and photos from his immensely varied life and career. In an old dusty leather case he found a long-forgotten scrapbook, a medley of documentation relating to the task he had taken on all those years ago corroborating his incredible deed. Next to it lay a list of names and particulars of 669 children; each entry representing a life he had saved. Such papers could not be thrown away – they were people's lives.

Grete was astonished. Incredibly, her husband had not told her of his achievement. For all those years he had kept it to himself. 'It happened so long ago', he said as he gazed at the pile in front of him. 'Quite frankly, I haven't given that episode much thought since. It didn't seem that important.'

Not that important? Of the 15,000 Czech Jewish children taken to the camps, only a tiny fraction returned. Winton had, therefore, saved the major part of my generation of Czech Jews. How many men can boast of a feat of such magnitude? But Winton is a modest, private man; to boast, to draw attention to himself, is certainly not in his nature.

Whilst trying to find a suitable home for his papers, inevitably, the story broke and in February 1988 featured in the *Sunday Mirror*. Simultaneously, Esther Rantzen's television programme *That's Life* was presented in which I was the first Winton child to be introduced to him. I could not believe my good fortune when Esther's researchers telephoned and asked me to take part in the programme together with several other Winton children and told me who I was going to meet. My hopes, my dreams of finding my saviour, would at last come true! I have no words to describe how I felt, sitting next to the man to whom I owe so much, being able to embrace him and, at long last, to thank him for my life.

To add to my joy and to the list of coincidences, Winton's sudden appearance could not have come at a more opportune moment, for I had found a publisher for my autobiography. The manuscript was actually at the printers when we met at the television studios, but I was able to add some details of his involvement in our rescue in the introduction to my story. A few months later, when I had driven the short distance from my cottage to his home (another coincidence, we live just a few miles apart), it meant a great deal to me to present him with the first copy of *Pearls of Childhood*. Without him I would not be here to tell the tale.

Since our initial meeting in 1988 several small and some larger reunions of Winton children have taken place in Britain, the Czech Republic, the USA and Israel and honours have been bestowed upon him in recognition of his deed. There seems to be a forever-growing interest in his story and much acclaim comes to him from all corners of the world. But the letters and visits he receives from those whose lives he had saved so long ago mean more to him than all the acclaim. Up to now, more than 250 of 'his' children have been in touch. A warm welcome always awaits them in the Winton home. Until her death in September 1999, Grete's warmth, hospitality and friendliness were much appreciated.

With pitifully few exceptions, all of us Winton children had lost our parents and most of our extended family; some had lost siblings who were left behind. The Holocaust had deprived not only us, but our children of grandparents, cousins, aunts and uncles and old family friends. Is it any wonder that this kind, compassionate man to whom we owe so much has become a much loved father-figure, even a grandfather-figure of a very large family?

All this has, of course, led to an even greater pile of papers accumulating than the one he attempted to dispose of back in 1987 and has certainly not helped towards an uneventful, peaceful retirement. Sometimes he grumbles about it, but I always see a glint of pride, satisfaction and pleasure in his eyes.

Winton still shakes his head in bewilderment and disbelief when compared to Oskar Schindler and Raoul Wallenberg. I try to make him realise that his contribution to the human race is immeasurable.

WHO WILL SAVE THE CHILDREN?

On his frequent trips to Germany during the years preceding World War II, Winton watched with apprehension the growing strength of the Nazis and the effect their propaganda was having on the people. He saw families divided amongst themselves, Jews being beaten and arrested and the ruthless aggressiveness of the SS. He could hardly believe how all the evidence of the build-up of totalitarianism could be shrugged off by Britain, especially when Hitler's troops set off on their march across Europe in March 1938, when Austria was the first country to be incorporated into the German Reich. Hitler then set his sights on the Sudetenland – strategically the most vital region on the Czech–German border – making his usual pronouncement that this was to be his last territorial ambition.

The Czechoslovak government turned to Britain and France for help. When, in 1918, the Republic of Czechoslovakia was founded, both countries had signed treaties guaranteeing assistance if ever the republic was attacked. The Czechs were, therefore, confident; their army ranked amongst the best in the world and Sudetenland had the strongest belt of fortifications in Europe – and they had sworn allies. Yet, when Hitler threatened war unless his demands for the acquisition of the Sudetenland were met, the allies chose to believe his assurances that his appetite would be appeased. As September 1938 was drawing to a close, they caved in to Hitler's ultimatum at the Munich Conference and pressured the Czechoslovak government to surrender the Sudetenland to Germany without a fight. To the Czech people, this was a betrayal; to Neville Chamberlain, the British Prime Minister, a victory. He called the Munich crisis 'a quarrel in a faraway country between people we know nothing about ...'. A small price to pay for world peace. Sadly, most of Europe agreed with him.

The annexation of the Sudetenland caused thousands of people to flee into what remained of Czechoslovakia, particularly to areas in and around Prague. Many were already refugees from Germany and Austria, now fleeing for the second time. Some were Poles and Hungarians, as their countries also took a slice each of the border regions whilst the Germans helped themselves to the Sudetenland. But whether Czech, Austrian or German, they were all racial or political enemies of the Third Reich: social democrats, communists, prominent literary figures and other intellectuals – most were Jews. With the exception of a fortunate few with personal contacts, the refugees were housed in makeshift camps where they existed, often in appalling conditions, without any means of support.

Meanwhile, in Germany hate and violence against the Jews was growing daily, culminating in the *Kristallnacht* pogrom on 9 November 1938 when Jewish homes, shops, businesses and synagogues were destroyed, hundreds murdered, thousands arrested. This latest turn of events convinced the bulk of refugees sheltering in Czechoslovakia, many resident Jews and prominent anti-fascist figures that it was only a matter of time before Hitler invaded the now defenceless remaining part of the country and they were desperate to get out of his reach.

The brutality of *Kristallnacht* showed the world all too clearly that Jews under Nazi rule had no future. The British government, under pressure from a radicalised public opinion and the leaders of the Council for German Jewry, relaxed their immigration laws. This generous gesture was in sharp contrast to the conclusions reached at the Evian Conference, held on the shores of Lake Geneva, back in July 1938. Although government representatives of the 31 countries present voiced much sympathy for the beleagured Jews of Nazi Germany, they were eager to justify only their reasons for not increasing immigration quotas. Their internal problems, such as unemployment and depression in Britain, seemed significantly more important than the fate of the Jews. Yet now, four months later, the British government gave the go-ahead for a then unspecified number of endangered children from Germany and Austria to enter Britain with a simplified travel document and a collective guarantee, on the condition that they would not be a drain on the public purse.

Under the umbrella of the Refugee Children's Movement (The Movement) – a subsidiary group of the Central British Fund for World Jewish Relief – various voluntary organisations, such as the Society of Friends (Quakers), the Jewish Refugee Committee, the Inter-Aid Committee and many concerned individuals, Jewish and Christian, pulled together to organise 'Operation *Kindertransport*'.

With the expectation of a large influx of refugees, an intensive fund-raising effort had to be made. This was achieved by the setting up of the Earl Baldwin Fund, launched in early December 1938, when Stanley Baldwin issued the following radio appeal: 'I ask you to come to the aid of victims not of any catastrophe in the natural world, not of earthquake, not of flood, not of famine, but of an explosion of Man's inhumanity to Man.'

The public responded generously and in a matter of six months the fund rose to half a million pounds, £220,000 of which was set aside for children under the care of The Movement. Until that time, Jewish refugees were almost totally supported by funds raised by the Jewish community. Gifts for the children poured in, not only clothing and equipment, but offers of accommodation, such as farms, hostels, empty holiday camps and houses.

The first group arrived on 3 December 1938; the last, from an orphanage in Amsterdam, on 14 May 1940. The few who were guaranteed went to their relatives or foster-parents. The others, from infants to teenagers, were packed into hastily converted holiday camps and hostels which provided temporary accommodation until permanent places could be found in private homes, Jewish and gentile, in schools and hostels, or on Zionist agricultural training farms. By the time war was declared on 3 September 1939, almost 10,000 children up to the age of 17 years had been rescued. These arrangements concerned the children who came directly from Austria and Germany. But what about the threatened children in Czechoslovakia? The year 1938 was drawing to its close. Who was there to organise *their* mass evacuation?

ENTER MR WINTON

Winton recollects:

It all happened during a short telephone conversation one Friday evening in December 1938. I was due to leave for Switzerland on the following Monday, for a skiing holiday with my friend, Martin Blake, a master at Westminster School. He rang me and simply said 'I have cancelled my holiday and I hope you'll do the same. I am off to Prague. I have the most interesting assignment and I need your help. I am in a tearing rush and can't go into details now, but my address will be Hotel Sroubek, Prague. Come as soon as you can.'

Martin and I had been friends for many years and had been on many winter-sports holidays together. We had a great number of interests in common and we were both very politically minded and very left wing. We spent hours discussing politics, in particular the growing menace of Hitler's Germany which we both felt would bring war. I felt certain that this Prague mission of his was connected with Hitler. It shows the strength of our friendship that, without probing further, I too cancelled my holiday and booked my flight to Prague for the following Tuesday, just before Christmas 1938. Late that night, I arrived at Hotel Sroubek. Martin was in bed, but not yet asleep. He told me about the refugees who had fled from the Sudetenland into Czechoslovakia ahead of Hitler's army. Martin was an emissary from the British Committee for Refugees from Czechoslovakia (BCRC) which was trying to get out of the country the adults who were in the greatest danger as fast as they could get them jobs, permits and people to guarantee them. The movement had already started, but left one major problem unresolved: THE CHILDREN ...

There were children whose parents had left them behind, others who were orphaned and children whose parents were desperate to get them at least to safety, because they themselves

66

were unable to leave; they were told that a job would be more likely to be found in Britain if they did not apply as a family.

Since the Munich crisis the BCRC had an office in Prague, headed by Doreen Warriner. Aided by her young secretary, Bill Barazetti, they worked to the point of exhaustion to help the refugees survive in the appalling conditions and to get the adults who were in greatest danger to safety. A few concerned individuals and agencies were involved in bringing out children singly, or in small groups, but there was no one to provide the skeleton for the existing agencies, no one to take on the responsibility of organising a mass exodus of the endangered children. That is, no one until Winton arrived on the scene.

Winton soon realised that he was earmarked for solving the problem and that the hopes of thousands of parents would be pinned on him. He could have just walked away, or could have offered to help in some small way – after all, the plight of the children was not his concern. But he always had sympathy for the underdog, the outsider, and was by nature compassionate, adventurous and never one to reject a challenge. All this, coupled with his awareness of the dangers, fuelled his willingness to help. His plan of action was deceptively simple: think large! think positive! never believe it can't be done! never give in! He did not hesitate and accepted to take on this mammoth, life-saving task.

Winton's decision marked the beginning of his lifelong humanitarian activities; his interest in helping mankind was born at that moment and is with him still to this day. Winton recollects:

> The task of assessing the problem was enormous. There were thousands of children needing help. Doreen Warriner had sent out the cry for help and was, therefore, the person to help me collect the information I required and so I spent the first day in her office where anyone who needed help was welcome; there was a continual queue to see her. After a few days this applied to me as well. My day usually started with interviews in my bedroom whilst I was shaving (sometimes at 6.00am). Some parents said that they

would willingly take the risk of staying in the country if we could only find some way of getting their children to safety. A few had plenty of money, others not the price of a meal. Those with small children in their arms could not bear the thought of being parted from them. Some relief could be given with money, but our resources were very limited. Many required clothing as it was bitterly cold and here we were greatly helped by Mr Sams who was the Prague representative of the Lord Mayor's Fund, which had been set up in London to help such people. Some of their questions were unanswerable. If Doreen told the parents that she could get them to safety, but not the children, there was weeping and there was also weeping when we had to say that, at the moment, we could help neither parents nor children. And there was more weeping when we told the parents that if their children were found places in England, we could not guarantee if, or when, they would be reunited. It was all quite overwhelming. Some of the mothers were already on the 'streets' to get money to buy food for themselves and their families. I felt quite dazed. What suffering there is when armies start to march!

The size of the problem I had volunteered to help with started to emerge. I realised that a list of the most urgent cases would have to be made. There were five committees in Prague dealing with separate sections of refugees: Jewish, Catholic, Communist, Austrian and German, and politically exposed writers. Each group felt that they were the most urgent and that their particular priority would be lost if one master list was made. But one list was essential. After two days hard work appealing to these committees to co-operate, the position seemed hopeless. I was on my own – those dealing with the adults were far too busy even to talk to me. I telephoned all five committees and said that one list had been submitted to me and that unless I received the others within 24 hours, that would be the one I would use. This strategy worked and with the aid of all committees, a master list was compiled and it was this list, which although continuously kept up to date and altered as new information was received, was the one from which the children were eventually chosen.

It was at this time that I came upon a map (which I still have) setting out the dates when Hitler intended to annex the various countries of Europe. It was not believed. The map, which also forecast the eventual partitioning of France, could hardly be believed even once war had started. I worked very hard to protect my nerves and treated, as far as I was able, the whole operation on a purely business basis.

On the way out to Prague I had met a businessman called Mr Hales (who told me that he had initiated the Blue Ribbon for crossing the Atlantic) and I told him where I was staying. He turned up one morning and was much surprised to find the kind of work I was engaged in. I was just off to visit one of the refugee camps outside Prague and as there was room in the car he said he would like to come too. Miss Eleanor Rathbone, MP, was one of the party and I was told to keep an eye on her as she was always leaving things behind. The camp was unbelievably wretched and squalid. When I was in the third hut, I realised my business friend was missing. I went back and found him lying in one of the beds in the first hut, crying. I realised then, more certainly than ever, that if I was to achieve anything, I would have to protect myself from being torn asunder by each individual case of hardship and misery. I collected Eleanor Rathbone's handbag which she had left behind and we returned to Prague in a snowstorm.

Eleanor Rathbone was entirely dedicated to the refugee cause. She triggered support amongst other intellectuals and Members of Parliament and ensured that the refugee question was raised in the House of Commons again and again.

A few days later I was snatching a quick sandwich with Doreen, when I mentioned that I had a curious feeling that I was being followed. Doreen said 'of course you are being followed, so am I and all members of my staff'. She explained that she was, after all, trying to evacuate people whom the Nazis were looking for and that Prague was teeming with Nazi agents. I told Doreen that I had met a girl who was the representative of the Swedish Red Cross and had authority to arrange the transport of 20 children to Sweden. All three of us met for lunch the following day. Doreen and the Swedish girl seemed to be carrying on a lively conversation, but as I started to say something about our work, I got a kick from Doreen. She quickly changed the subject and we were engaged in various small talk until the meal was over. As we parted, she whispered 'go easy'. Doreen's suspicions had been roused and, as she had contacts everywhere, she checked with the Swedish Embassy and found out that the girl was working for the Germans. I was to have nothing more to do with her. However, her 'cover' as representative of the Swedish Red Cross was in order and I decided to be careful, but to go ahead. A week later, I was at the airport when the first transport of 20 children left for Sweden. Doreen was delighted. As an unofficial person with no status, I could step in where she was not allowed to tread.

A young Englishman met me in my hotel one day. Trevor Chadwick had heard about the plight of the refugees and offered to throw up his job as a teacher and come out to help. Two days after our meeting, he flew back to England with two refugee boys for his mother to look after. The next day he was back in Prague and from then on worked with me for about 18 hours a day until we both returned to England. Later, when we had got things moving in London and I needed someone to look after the Prague end, I took up Trevor's offer. I became so absorbed in this work in Prague that I forgot at times that I was on holiday from my firm in the city. There were meetings, interviews, visits to the camps and then more meetings. With luck, I was in bed by 1.00am and there was no need for an alarm clock, as someone would surely knock at my door early to plead the case of some child being put on the priority list I was compiling.

I wrote to my boss, as did Doreen Warriner, pleading for at least an extra week to enable me to finish the work.

Letter from Doreen Warriner to Mr Hart, dated 11 January 1939:

Mr Winton is, as you know, working with the refugee organisations here and has taken over the organisation of the child emigration. This is now at a very critical point and if he leaves at the moment, I am afraid the whole thing would come to a standstill; could he not possibly remain another two weeks? I am relying on him to organise the chaos which exists here and then to bring the documents to London. I am very shorthanded and have no one else who can take over the work he is doing. It really is esential if the plans are to go through.

You must excuse my request, but I would not make it if it really did not seem very important for the work to be carried over this difficult point. I am extremely grateful to you for letting Mr Winton come, his energy is absolutely invaluable and he has drawn all the different organisations together in a most amazing way and brought order into the chaos, and got plans for child emigration to Sweden on a big scale, so I do hope you will not mind my asking if he can remain till he can hand it over.

Winton still has the grudging reply to their request:

CREWS & CO.
30 Throgmorton Street,
London, E.C.2.   9th January 1939

I have returned today to the city after a nice holiday at my new villa in the South of France. There is very little doing in the Kaffir market, but I would sooner you were taking a rest here rather than doing heroic work with thousands of poor devils who are suffering through no fault of their own. You are more experienced than Cooke and there is always something in a small way to be done and to study.

For instance, I still think Western Holdings will go lower – probably West Wits and Western Reef also. There is so much new capital required, both in South and West Africa, that there is little chance of good markets while all this fresh money has to be found.

Mr Chamberlain's visit, we all hope, will produce some good and if this is the case, we hope you will be able to get back to the office by Monday.

With best wishes for the New Year and may it be more profitable for you than the last.

Yours sincerely,

(signed) J. Geoffrey Hart

Winton adds rather sadly,

I went to see this same gentleman after the Dunkirk evacuation. He greeted me by saying: 'It is really no damn good to carry on. We should try and make peace with Hitler now and see what we can save from the wreck.' If the Germans had ever arrived, we should have had our quislings.

Despite all this, I stayed on in Prague for another ten days. The last week was more hectic than ever. I was then 29, strong and active and rather enjoyed the pace at which I had to work. Whilst there, I met a very wonderful person called the Reverend Rosalind Lee. She was the head of the Unitarian Church in England and had come out to see what she could do to help. She was horrified at the situation. When we both got back home, she gave me £100 she had collected in her church, which at that time was a great help. But the greatest help she gave me was her confidence in my ability to succeed. I still have the articles she wrote in *The Inquirer* dated 15.4.1939.

There are many articles, letters and other entries in Winton's scrapbook which confirm, in greater detail, Winton's efforts whilst in Prague and after his return to England. They also illustrate how much teamwork was needed, and given, by others involved in this rescue operation. Most are too faded to reproduce, such as the following letter written by Doreen Warriner to Margaret Layton (Honorary Secretary of BCRC in London) when Winton was about to return to London:

January 20th 1939

Dear Miss Layton,

Could I suggest that you put the organisation of the children refugees from Czechoslovakia in the hands of Winton? He is ideal for the job. He has enormous energy, business methods, knows the situation perfectly well here.

He has prepared the case sheets of several hundred of the children, collected all the offers and all that he needs now is authority to go ahead. It is an opportunity for the committee to get the services of a really first class organiser.

I've been trying for three months to get these children away, Save the Children has disclaimed responsibity, so has InterAid and our own committee is overburdened with more urgent things. I would be glad if I could delegate this part of the work as I am sure you would. It could quite well be taken out of the committee's scope, and Winton will get things through, if you will give him status as secretary of a children's section.

Our main difficulty is that *we do not know how to get permits through the H.O.*

We now have complete case sheets for 760 cases with photographs and complete data.

NEVER SAY IT CAN'T BE DONE

Winton returned to London armed with hundreds of photos and details of children who were on his priority list. He was not over-optimistic about the outcome of Doreen Warriner's letter. He was well aware that the BCRC was far too heavily

73

committed, already coping with endangered adults and was, therefore, not unduly surprised when his meetings with Margaret Layton came to nothing. He fared no better when he turned to The Movement, which spearheaded the *kindertransports* from Germany and Austria. As many of Winton's most urgent cases were German and Austrian refugee children from the camps, it made no sense to him that his request for their inclusion was turned down. The Movement, funded mainly by the Baldwin Fund, blamed insufficient resources for their negative responses; their workload and finances were stretched to the limit.

Winton was undeterred. The simplest and most effective way to proceed would have been to work through an existing organisation, as he had hoped, but this was not to be. He also knew that he would not get very far without an official status and, as the BCRC were dragging their feet in giving him one, he took the matter into his own hands.

> When one is an employee, one does what one is told or risks losing one's job. This leads to a certain amount of caution and a great deal of hypocrisy. Happily, I had no such constraints. Luckily the Stock Exchange closed at 3.30pm and I had plenty of free time. As a start, I had notepaper printed with the name of the British Committee for Refugees from Czechoslovakia, under which, in bold type, was **The Children's Section** and then my private address. This looked official and impressive.

Then began the bureaucratic battle before the actual rescue could begin. The first step was to tackle the Home Office. At that time, what remained of Czechoslovakia was still free territory and the authorities, though sympathetic, were complacent about the impending threat of Hitler's armies. 'What is the hurry?', they would ask. 'Nothing else is going to happen in Europe.' Perhaps it was this conviction and the fact that Winton was out on his own without a strong financial backer to fund block guarantees which resulted in more stringent terms of entry for 'his' children than for the child refugees who were coming through The Movement direct from Germany and Austria, hundreds at a time, many even without a guarantee. In their case, if the financial responsibility for maintenance, education and training could not be provided by other groups or individuals it was usually funded, as stated earlier, by the Baldwin Fund.

Winton was not an official part of a large organisation and had no means to fund such a venture, so his task was more complicated. Before an entry permit was issued, he had to submit a separate application for each child, together with a medical certificate and proof that the youngster had a home to go to and a guarantor or foster-parent willing to keep and educate him up to the age of 17 years. Furthermore, a deposit of £50 had to be put up to cover the cost of eventual return to the child's homeland, or re-emigration to the Dominions, colonies or Palestine. As the annual wage averaged less than £500, such a sum was well above most people's means.

In April 1939, the British government decided to restrict the influx of child refugees and imposed the same conditions as on the Winton children, on children coming under the auspices of The Movement. By then, thousands had already been brought over from Germany and Austria. Once again the Baldwin Fund agreed to foot the bill for maintenance or re-emigration deposits for children who had no guarantors, or whose families could not afford to pay. Winton recalls that The Movement also took and placed 40 of 'his' children.

Winton was well aware, right from the start, that before his life-saving mission could really get under way, he would have to find a way round any obstacle and that if he wanted to succeed, he would have to use all his incentive, work hard and at speed.

As soon as I had my own stationery printed, I started writing to organisations and the press, asking for their help in finding guarantors and foster-parents. Then I had a stroke of luck. Barbara Willis, a young friend of Martin Blake, who was working for one of the Christian refugee organisations, turned up at my home one evening and offered her secretarial services. Moreover, she gave me a complete list of all the British Committee's contacts throughout the country. She said 'You have taken over the British Committee's name unofficially, you have formed a Children's Section unofficially, you have called yourself Honorary Secretary unofficially; you may as well finish the job by taking over all the British Committee's local societies.' And so the 'business' really got started. We drafted a document giving full details of the desperate position in Czechoslovakia making an urgent case for rescuing the children. We stated that we had a list of 500 most urgent cases and particulars of the children with photographs could be made available to any would-be guarantors. This information was sent to all the local societies of the BCRC and the result was astonishing. We were, at last, in business.

To get the best results, Winton had cards printed, each with the photos of six children with their names and ages from which prospective foster-parents or guarantors could choose. Some people objected to such a measure saying that it made the whole venture seem horribly commercial, but seeing the photos helped enormously to place the children and that was what mattered most. Eventually there were four people dealing with the work; Winton joined them every day at about 4.00pm and worked until all hours.

Lists of the children for whom homes had been found and guarantees obtained were submitted to the Home Office. Sometimes the lack of urgency and understaffing resulted in the Aliens Department being so slow in issuing the entry permits, that Trevor Chadwick, who by then was in charge of organising the exodus of children at the Prague end, or Bill Barrazetti (Doreen Warriner's secretary) had to forge the documents. Surprisingly, the Czechs and later the Germans accepted and stamped the faked documents, unaware they were not genuine. The British would not have been so gullible and Winton always sent someone to the port of entry to unobtrusively substitute the fake permits with the genuine ones, which had by then been received.

There was still a great deal of work to be done in Prague before a transport could leave. Exit and transit permits had to be obtained for all the children, special coaches and later entire trains had to be booked and paid for and the selected children brought to Prague on or before the stipulated day. Reliable adults also had to be found to look after the children whilst in transit. Such carers had to be relied on to return to Prague. Had any absconded, it would have put all future transports in jeopardy. Sometimes a teenager, too old to be included as one of the children, took on the role of carer and was able to remain in England provided the papers were in order and employment guaranteed.

Early in March, Winton submitted the first list of 20 children for whom homes and sponsors had been secured. Doreen Warriner was delighted as is obvious from her letter:

Prague, March 6 1939

British Committee for Refugees from Czechoslovakia.

Dear Nicky,

I do congratulate you most sincerely in this great achievement, and know what an effort it must have been. I am so glad the sword never rested in your hand.

I am going to ask Chadwick and Lehmann to select the children.

There are a great number of things I want to write about, but the chief thing is to congratulate you and I must wait till times are quieter; today is a bad time and I have already reduced many harmless people to tears.

Yours,
Doreen

That first, relatively small group of Winton children left on 14 March 1939 – one day before German troops invaded and occupied what remained of Czechoslovakia!

* * *

When Hitler broke his pledge to honour Czechoslovakia's new frontiers and his troops poured into the country, it took just one day for him to reach Prague's Hradcany Castle and announce to the stricken nation that their republic had now become the Protectorate of Bohemia and Moravia – a colony of the great Reich. The Slovaks had autonomy, but they had to adhere to the policies of their German masters. The leader of their government was a Catholic priest, Josef Tiso, an ardent fascist and anti-Semite, who seemed more than willing to co-operate. Later, when the deportation of Jews to the death camps began, Tiso even offered to pay the Germans per capita for every Jew taken off his hands and, in addition, supplied the trains. After the war he was executed as a traitor, but later, as racism in Slovakia took hold, he was lauded as a national hero!

In the spring of 1939, however, after the German occupation, there was at first no visible violence towards Jews. Hitler was anxious, at least for the time being, to try to convince the world that he was quite a decent chap, but behind the scenes there were many arrests, particularly of the known political enemies of the Reich. Thousands were rounded up from the local population and the refugee camps – whatever their creed. Most of them were taken to German concentration camps.

It was obvious to the world that Hitler's word could not be trusted, that his greed would not be appeased and that peace – even peace at any price – could not be bought, as Chamberlain had hoped. The threat of war was very real now; it could no longer be ignored.

Winton had no illusions about what lay ahead. He guessed war was imminent and that there was no time to lose. Rescuing endangered children now took on extra urgency and he doubled his efforts, seeking help wherever he could. His attempts to reach as many members of the public as possible paid dividends and his network of contacts grew steadily. Before long, numerous British voluntary missions and agencies of goodwill, some of which were already involved in the rescue of children from Germany and Austria, began to work hand in hand with Winton and his team. Appeals were placed in newspapers and magazines, on radio, in synagogues and churches; he contacted schools and institutes, any group or agency that came to mind. There was a steady flow of offers of homes and sponsors, not only from individual Jews and Jewish organisations, but notably from many Christian families and institutions; from the clergy, teachers, doctors and dentists, and architects and taxi drivers. The middle class were the most generous, but others, rich and poor, joined the fight to snatch young lives from Hitler's clutches.

LIFE IS A LOTTERY

The recent turn of events made the plight of the refugees in the protectorate more desperate than anyone could imagine. Prior to the occupation they had managed to keep just one step ahead of Hitler's army; now they were trapped and, for most, there was no escape. Foreign embassies in Prague were now besieged by terrified asylum-seekers fearing for their lives and the lives of their families. Czechs, foreigners, Jewish and Aryan were in danger. Panic, terror and suicides became a common occurrence.

Although no one was aware at that time to what length Hitler would go to try to wipe the Jewish population off the face of Europe, the shadow of *Kristallnacht*, the threatening rumours of persecution, the sudden stigma of being a Jew and the fear of the unknown future hung like heavy black clouds over our household and thousands of others.

The queues in front of the BCRC office were now unending. Parents, who until then could not face the thought of separation, became increasingly desperate to send their children to a safe haven, despite the heartbreak such a separation would bring.

Before the occupation, hundreds of Czechs, mostly Jews, queued with the refugees, hoping their child would be accepted. Now, they came in their thousands – my mother amongst them. She had heard about Winton's efforts and the transports. Unknown to the rest of the family, she took steps to do everything possible to get my elder sister and me to safety. I shall never forget my father's shocked face when she told him we had both been selected – how old and haggard he suddenly looked. We all waited in silence until, at last, he smiled at us with tears in his eyes, sighed and said 'alright, let them go'.

79

It is impossible to imagine how the parents must have felt, hoping, yet fearing, that out of the thousands of names their child or children would be chosen. What courage and strength was necessary and a special kind of unselfish love, to make the ultimate sacrifice to part with their child. How hard it must have been to go through with their decision, to let them go to a faraway country, to complete strangers, without even knowing the language. Would the foster-parents be kind to their beloved children? Would they love them? But the questions which must have weighed most heavily on their minds were the same for every parent. Will our separation be a lengthy one? Will we ever see each other again?

My own mother and father, as many other parents, did their best to be optimistic and cheerful when told that both my sister and I had been chosen to go to England. They had no plans – nor opportunity – to follow us. My maternal grandmother was blind, my grandfather an invalid. Mother would not contemplate leaving them behind. We kept telling ourselves that war might yet be averted and that, if it did break out, it would be of short duration, with the allies the victors. 'Let us hope that it is all a storm in a teacup', my father used to say. 'You'll be back within a year, you'll see', he kept repeating, as if to convince himself. Had we admitted to ourselves that we might never see each other again, I doubt we could have parted.

Some children, particularly the little ones, were told that they were going on holiday, that their mummy and daddy would follow soon. Some of the older ones looked upon the trip as an adventure, coupled with the opportunity to get to know another country, to learn another language. Those in their teens were more apprehensive, less certain that there would be a happy reunion.

When the time came to say goodbye many children cried, reaching out to their parents, pleading not to be sent away, feeling bewildered, deserted. The scene at Prague station, late at night on 29 June 1939 will be with me for ever. The special train with 241 children – my sister and I amongst them – the forced cheerfulness of our parents – their last words of love, encouragement and advice. Until that moment, I felt more excited than afraid, but when the whistle blew and the train slowly pulled out of the station, my beloved mother and father could no longer mask their anguish. And I, feeling vulnerable and utterly lost, realised how lucky I was to have my sister at my side, not to be completely alone.

* * *

Winton's main concern was to place the children. The lifestyle and religion of the family had to be of secondary importance. In any case there were no social workers to check the suitability and no time to be selective. Saving young lives was all that mattered. It was heartening to see how many ordinary people responded to his pleas.

Not everyone approved of Winton's methods. The splitting up of siblings was a frequent objection. To this he replies:

> Remember, there was a recession in Britain; people were short of cash. Those who offered homes were mainly the lower middle-class. Taking one child was a phenomenal undertaking. Had I waited for families willing to take two or more, most of those children would not have got away.

It was fortunate that Winton felt this way as far as my sister and I were concerned and that our parents did not insist that the two of us must stay together. Eva went to an upper-class Church of England boarding school in an opulent town in the south with the headmistress acting as guardian, whilst I was fostered by a warm, devout, Methodist family in the north, with little money to spare but a big generous heart.

There were complaints that many of the children found their way into Christian homes and institutions, but there was a definite shortage of Jewish families and hostels in Britain prepared to offer alternative refuge to those needing help. One must bear in mind that by the time the transports from Prague got going, thousands of children from Germany had already arrived and, consequently, most of the places available within the Jewish community had been taken.

Winton explained:

> I am not religious. I didn't mind whether the children were Jewish, Communist, Catholic or whatever and I didn't mind who they went to. I think one of the points which is overlooked, particularly by the Jews, is that at least 10 per cent of the children brought out to England had non-Jewish parents who had stuck out their necks politically.

Although many members of the Anglo-Jewish community devoted their time and effort and gave financial assistance to the refugee children's cause, there were others who preferred to ignore their existence, or offered, often reluctantly, minimal help. On the other hand, Jewish schools, hostels, training farms and other organisations accepted as many children as they could accommodate and ensured that they kept their Jewish identity. Winton recalls that B'nai B'rith – a Jewish fraternal society with hostels in and around London – was particularly helpful.

Probably the most active organisation was Children and Youth Aliyah. After *Kristallnacht*, this Zionist group, which was supported by private grants and donations raised, for example, through the British Council of the Young Pioneer Movement for Palestine and the Eddie Cantor Appeal, set up agricultural training centres in various parts of Britain. Hundreds of Jewish boys and girls in the 14–17 age group (the most difficult to place in families) were accommodated in such centres. Foster-parents generally preferred children between six and ten years old, particularly girls. On these special farms, where there was strict discipline and very few home comforts, the children lived, studied and worked collectively. Everything possible was done to avoid their being placed in a non-Jewish environment with possible exposure to conversion. The purpose of these centres was to combine agricultural training with educational and Zionist values – the ultimate goal being to prepare the youngsters for a pioneering life in villages and agricultural settlements in Palestine, once war ended.

One such centre was at Great Egham Farm in Kent which was given to Youth Aliyah following an appeal in a London newspaper. Amongst the German and Austrian children living there, approximately 150 in all, were 25 youngsters who came on Winton's transports from Prague. As the war continued and the children grew up, most left and were replaced by others who had reached the required age.

Just as Youth Aliyah was intent on ensuring that the children kept and developed their Jewish identity, there were some organisations, mainly the Barbican Mission, whose aim was to bring the children up in the Christian tradition and ultimately convert them.

Inevitably, there was quite an outcry, particularly from the orthodox rabbis, against bringing children to Britain under such conditions. Some went to see Winton in his office to lodge a personal protest, which he ignored:

> I took no notice of their objections. It may seem terrible from the Jewish point of view but, on the other hand, the children are alive! I was after saving lives, not souls. I told them: 'I've got my work to do, you've got yours. If you prefer a dead Jew to a proselytised one, that's your business.'

The Barbican Mission to the Jews, whose teaching denounces anti-Semitism or any form of racism, was rescuing children from Czechoslovakia even before Winton appeared on the scene. In fact, the first transport Winton witnessed leaving Prague on 12 January 1939 consisted entirely of children, some as young as three or four years, selected by Reverend B. Walner, who represented the Mission in Prague. According to Harry, who was one of the children on the plane, the Reverend Walner had baptised some of them before they left for England, obviously with their parents' consent. As confirmed in Winton's scrapbook the only role the BCRC played on that occasion was to arrange and pay for the transport.

The second Barbican air transport arrived in Britain a week before Hitler marched into Prague. It was accompanied by the

Reverend Davidson who, with his wife and other caring helpers, looked after the children in the Houses of Refuge in Chislehurst and later in Devon. There were now 50 children in the Mission's care. As time went on and more children destined for the Mission arrived on Winton's *kindertransports*, the number rose to a hundred, some of the children coming originally from Germany and Poland.

According to Mrs Davidson's recollections in *The House of Refuge in England* (Mount Zion, Chislehurst, 1978, private publication), the Mission was prepared to take in some 80 more children, but by then certain sections of orthodox Jews dug in their heels and succeeded in holding back their departure, although written consent to conversion of the children had been given by the parents. The objections to proselytisations were understandable, yet they resulted in tragic consequences for most of these children whose escape route was thus barred and their fate sealed.

Although the majority of the children who came to the Mission were Jewish, some were of mixed marriages; most came from non-religious homes. It must have seemed utterly alien and bewildering to them – apart from being uprooted and taken to a foreign land, suddenly to find Bible studies and church at the centre of their lives. Harry recalls,

> It was quite a shock, a completely different life. The first seven nights spent on a mattress in the church hall, straight to a local school and into the church choir. No physical pressure was ever used to make us join in Christian worship, but Daddy Davidson (as we were asked to call him) got quite shirty if we didn't pay attention at the prayer meetings which were held twice a day and if we didn't accept Jesus as our personal saviour.

There is no doubt that most of the parents, in their anxiety to get their children to safety, gave permission for their conversion from Judaism because they dared not refuse any opportunity, whatever the conditions. Some may have thought that their child, as a Christian, might have an easier life in this anti-Semitic world. A large proportion of the children became practising Christians and have remained so to this day. There are those who feel that the conditions of acceptance were morally wrong, but each survivor will be forever grateful for the care given and for their life being saved.

The Barbican Mission placed emphasis not only on religion, but also on training and education, particularly if the child was gifted. I can think of no finer example than the story of twin brothers, Joseph and Peter Schneider, who came to the Mission at the age of ten. As their parents perished in the Holocaust, they remained in the care of the Mission even after the war. Joseph went on to study medicine, specialising in eye surgery, and worked for many years as a medical missionary in Africa. He died in 1997, leaving a widow and children. His brother Peter entered the Church and was, first, chaplain of a college at Cambridge University, then of a church in Haifa and, later, canon of the Anglican Cathedral in Jerusalem. His knowledge of Hebrew and Judaism was extensive; he could have put many a modern rabbi to shame. He never disclaimed his Jewish background; all his life he felt as much a Jew as a Christian.

I met Peter some years ago, when he was the vicar of Burpham in Sussex, but his main duties were those of an adviser on inter-faith matters to the Archbishop of Canterbury. As the Archbishop's envoy he travelled extensively, particularly to Israel; he worked tirelessly to bring greater understanding and unity. The high esteem in which he was held by the theological community was reflected in the memorial service held in Westminster Abbey after his untimely death in 1982. The Archbishops of York and Canterbury both officiated; the lesson from the Old Testament was read by the late Rabbi Hugo Gryn, himself a camp survivor of Czech origin. Christians, Jews and Moslems sat side by side at this thanksgiving service for the life and work of Peter Schneider, Christian by religion, Jewish by birth, who had come to these shores as a small refugee boy.

How can one evaluate the contribution to the human race made by these two brothers, raised by the Barbican Mission? They have more than repaid their debt for the saving of their lives and, perhaps, have more than justified Winton's attitude: better a converted Jew than a dead one.

THOSE WHO HELPED

The story of Winton's rescue mission would be incomplete if I did not include some of the people who joined the race against time to save young lives, as each person was a vital link in the ultimate success of the venture. Much has been writen about the exodus of children from Germany, but little about those from my country. There are few records available and recollections of the participants still alive today are, so long after the event, hazy, often inaccurate, and their testimonies conflicting. Without Winton's invaluable scrapbook and the list of children saved, it would have been very difficult, if not impossible to write these chapters. Happily, I have found some records to fill in the background.

I hope the reader will forgive any inaccuracies and omissions. I am no historian – just a Winton child grateful to be alive, a writer who is anxious and determined for this important part of history to be preserved and understood.

We Need Visas, Not Chocolate!

Without Doreen Warriner, there would be no story to tell. There is no doubt that she was the prime mover in setting up the whole project. Had she not cried for help to Martin Blake, had Blake not made that fateful phonecall to Winton, had Winton not responded, I dread to think what our fate would have been.

Warriner, a lecturer at the London School of Economics, flew to Prague in October 1938, shortly after the Munich crisis, with £150 donated for relief work by Save the Children Fund and £300 she had collected from friends and colleagues. 'I had no idea at all what to do, only a desperate wish to do something', she writes in her account 'Winter in Prague' (London, Imperial War Museum, unpublished manuscript, June 1939). This powerful and moving record of events describes mainly her work in organising the escape of the leaders of the Sudeten Social Democratic Party and, later on, of their wives and children, about 2,500 people in all. The exact number of refugees in Czechoslovakia at that time is not known; it may have run into six figures.

Initially, Warriner responded to the plight of the refugees by providing basic essentials with the little money she had been given; funds from other sources, such as the Lord Mayor's Fund and the News Chronicle Fund were very slow coming in. As the most urgent cases of the political refugees gradually left with the Labour Party's guarantee for financial support, their wives and children had to stay behind, under Warriner's care. At that time, she had no way of knowing if and when they could follow. This, coupled with the problem of children who were orphaned or whose parents had been arrested or lost in the chaos, prompted Warriner to send out the SOS to Blake. She describes how relieved she was when Winton appeared and took over the emigration of the children.

At the end of November 1938, Sir Walter Layton[1] came to Prague and asked Warriner to look after the News Chronicle Fund. 'He had distributed sums to various Czech refugee organisations and committees representing refugee groups, chief of which was HICEM, the Zionist organisation, headed by Frau Marie Šmolka', Warriner recalled. 'The BCRC, representing the Labour Party, the News Chronicle Fund and the Society of Friends, had been formed in London some time before, with Margaret Layton (Sir Walter's daughter) as secretary. Sir Walter asked me to act as their representative in Prague.'

Help from the Labour Party was centred, understandably, on those who were in most danger – eminent Social Democrats, members of parliament and trade union leaders. Warriner's frustration and concern for ordinary refugees in the camps, whom no one was helping, was growing by the day:

The morale in the camps was fading fast. Not many of the first 250 men came from the camps, yet most of the men there were anti-Henlein men who held a responsible position in their own town or village, where their former enemies were awaiting their return. For the camps, there was not a ray of hope and I could see no way of waking people at home to the need for visas. Plenty of organisations sent their representatives to help, but with the idea of giving relief, wool and chocolate. Emigration rather than relief was needed and visas, not chocolate. There was increasing danger and increasing despair.

Warriner, like Winton, was finding the British authorities difficult to deal with; they simply refused to grasp the danger and urgency of the situation. She writes:

> There was no longer any sense in discussing who was more in danger, because all democratic Germans were equally exposed. In Prague we lived on tenterhooks, but London was detached and calm. It was impossible to get through the cotton wool which prevented them from hearing.

In January a large loan fund was set up by the British government for the purpose of assisting the emigration and settlement of refugees who had fled into Czechoslovak territories. A special agreement stipulated that up to 5,000 Sudeten refugees should receive £200 per family to cover transport and resettlement. This 'generous gesture' which seemed like an act of contrition, was the result of long negotiations and, most importantly, it helped many refugees to reach Britain and other free countries on the Continent. It also enabled the Canadian government to offer refuge for up to 1,200 familes, on condition that money was there to back them. It is interesting to note that capitalist Canada was the only dominion country to open her doors. Labour-controlled Australia and New Zealand rejected all appeals for help. Even England at that time gave visas to the Sudeten refugees only on condition that the immigrants would not work and their sponsors guaranteed permanent support. One of the key personalities in securing the loan, which by the end of the war had helped 14,000 refugees, including many Winton children, was R.J. Stopford, of the Treasury, who was based in Prague at the British Legation. He had been a member of the Runciman Commission and it is largely thanks to him that the British government did acknowledge its obligation.

February was relatively a happy time. The most endangered refugees were gradually leaving and Winton's work started to show results. Warriner writes: 'He began to get his children's transports going; Trevor Chadwick, who took over the Prague end of the children's section from Winton, arranged a special plane for some of "my" children to be evacuated to England.'

She gives a vivid picture of the chaos, fear and misery which followed the Nazi occupation. She was particularly concerned about the fate of the wives and children of the 600 men who had already gone to England *en route* to Canada. In London, the BCRC had decided that they should remain in Czechoslovakia until the men departed for Canada in May or June, in order to save the cost of maintenance in England. 'This', said Stopford on 28 February, 'was the most refined form of charitable cruelty imaginable.' 'How cruel', Warriner adds, 'we did not yet know.'

By the end of March, the situation had become dangerous and it was vital to send the remaining women and children to safety. Warriner recalls that on the day a large group was about to leave she spent 'a happy hour with Trevor Chadwick packing food for seventy' which was followed, unhappily, by an appalling incident at the Wilson station where the Gestapo and their henchmen in the Secret Police rushed about in a frenzy, keeping the train waiting for hours.

> They came to terrorise, to reduce everyone to a state of helplessness and fear. There is no system, only a boiling cauldron into which every now and again a certain quantity of bones and blood must be thrown; it doesn't matter whose, but it does matter that those who are still free should see and tremble … There was no question of justice or mercy.

One woman and a Jew were taken off the train and were never heard of again. Trevor was also interrogated and said that he was helping Warriner.

Her position was becoming progressively more difficult and dangerous:

> There was a conflict between the two sides: to get caught in the illegal business (of evacuating the men through Poland

without adequate documention) quite certainly meant that the legal business on which the women and children depended would have to close down, and that the women would suffer.

In April, the Gestapo began arresting and interrogating some of Warriner's colleagues, including the remarkable Canadian Beatrice Wellington, who had worked all winter at the Czech Refugee Institute in Prague. Although she was questioned for two days runnning, six hours at a time, without being allowed to sit down, she stood up to the gruelling third degree interrogation splendidly. She told them nothing. They wanted information on the 'illegal business'.

It was obvious that Warriner's turn would be next; she was so heavily involved. This forced Stopford to suggest that it would be advisable for her to return to England as soon as possible. It was fortunate that she followed his advice. Five days after her departure, the Gestapo came to the BCRC office to arrest her.

In spite of her recent ordeal, Beatrice Wellingtion gladly took over Warriner's work. The last group of 120 women were still in Prague, desperate to leave. Wellington's task was far from easy; the Gestapo had become very suspicious of the Committee's activities. In a memorandum to Margaret Layton, sent at the end of May, she voiced her fears.

> Aiding political refugees to get to Poland illegally *en route* to England by whatever means at the Committee's disposal may not be considered illegal from the British point of view. It has already been made clear to me by the Gestapo that the British Committee's representative here, regardless who he or she is, will be promptly expelled from the country if found attempting to aid the women and children of men who have got to Poland illegally and are now in England or *en route* to England. A greater disaster resulting from this policy is that the case of the women and children themselves has been menaced and to date an increasing number of women are being imprisoned or are being subjected to mental torture because the records show that

their husbands have been aided in Poland ...

Unfortunately, the basis of our work and the possibility of continued negotiations to clear definite liabilities of the Committee have both been seriously – I am convinced fatally – prejudiced and injured by the recent discovery on the part of the German authorities of the Committee's work in Poland.

It is obviously quite impossible to negotiate legally here when a history of operations in Poland is before the Gestapo and is colouring their point of view. The most detrimental thing the Committee can continue to do, is to attempt to beat the Gestapo at their own game and expect a representative of the Committee to meet with any degree of co-operation from that body in Prague.

Nevertheless, Beatrice Wellington battled on in this sinister, dangerous atmosphere until the end of July, by which time she had managed to send the last group of 120 women and their children to safety.

* * *

One of the last entries in Warriner's account evaluates the work of Nicholas Winton and Trevor Chadwick:

Some children who were left alone because their mothers had been arrested I turned over to Chadwick to put on his big transports of Jewish children which he was now sending off to England through the Reich; a great mercy he and Nicky had been able to get these going. We talked on the terrace of the Legation where the magnolias were coming out in the sun against the dirty melting snow of March.

Who was this man who proved so valuable to Winton's mission of mercy? Two years Winton's senior, one of four children, Chadwick lost his father when only five years old. As a schoolboy, he was not always on his best behaviour, but he was clever and completed his studies at Oxford with a degree in jurisprudence – a subject thought to be useful for a career in the civil service. After a year in the Colonial Service in Nigeria, he married a farmer's daughter and went to teach at Forres, the preparatory school his father had founded in Swanage, Dorset.

Chadwick's uncle was the headmaster and he thought that his nephew would be just the person to take over the running of the school one day, but it soon became clear that he was far too much of a non-conformist for that. This tall, handsome, witty, unselfish young man proved to be an excellent teacher, but the job on its own lacked the stimulation he craved. Competitive sailing, fishing, gambling and whiling the nights away at the local pub helped to break up the monotony. It must have been difficult for his uncle, the headmaster, to have his nephew serving behind the bar, going out fishing at dawn, then turning up to teach still in his fisherman's jersey. Chadwick much preferred the company of the local fishing folk to that of the parents of his pupils and did his best to keep out of the way on parents' days. Whether to shock or amuse, once he turned up with his head shaven bare, and on another occasion, he posed as an ice-cream man selling ice-creams from a cart to the visitors as they walked up the drive! He detested convention in all its forms. But above all, he was remembered for his kindness; compassion and eagerness to help anyone in need far outweighed his faults and eccentricities. He was such a popular figure that after the war you could go to any pub in Swanage and people would gather round at the very mention of his name.

Trevor and his wife Marjorie had two sons, Charles, born in 1932 and William in 1934. They both recall a happy childhood in those early years, but life for their mother could hardly have been easy. When war loomed, everything changed utterly. What direction Chadwick's life would have taken had he not flown to Prague at the end of 1938 is hard to guess. One thing is certain; he would never have become headmaster of a respectable preparatory school!

It was fortunate indeed that Chadwick was sent to Prague with another master to bring back two refugee boys for the school to adopt. It must have been a heartbreaking task to select just two from so many deprived, threatened children. It is no wonder that Chadwick, like Winton, was quick to realise how badly and urgently help was needed. What a lucky coincidence that he heard of Winton's presence, that he sought him out and a partnership, which was to prove so significant to many lives, could be sealed!

Chadwick could have just selected the two boys who were to live with his family, his conscience appeased that he had done his share. He had no connections with Czechoslovakia, was not Jewish and was a thoroughbred Brit. But, like Winton, he was a humanitarian and thus he responded to the need and the challenge and volunteered to give up his job and help in the rescue. From then on, until their January return to London, the two men worked together, often into the night. 'We got a clear impression of the enormity of the task', Chadwick wrote in his account which appeared in Karen Gershon's book *We Came as Children* (Victor Golancz, 1966). 'We so often saw halls of confused refugees and batches of lost children, mostly Jewish, and we saw only the fringe of it all.'

Winton was impressed how well Chadwick coped and by the end of February, was pleased to take up Chadwick's offer to look after the Prague end. 'I knew he was the right man for the job', Winton said: 'He worked like a beaver, and when the Germans entered Prague in March he remained there and carried on under great difficulties.'

In Chadwick's account the months in Prague are vividly described:

I took my first air transport rather proudly, on a twenty-seater plane. They were all cheerfully sick, enticed by the little paper bags, except a baby of one who slept peacefully in my lap the whole time. Then there was the meeting with the guarantors – my baby was cooed over and hustled off, and the other nineteen were shyly summing up their new parents, faces alive with hope for the love they were obviously going to be given. I felt depressed as I returned to Prague. Only twenty! This was late that winter, early in 1939.

A member of the Czech cabinet lent me an office and I had two young helpers. The whole days, from 7 until 7, with twenty minutes for lunch, were taken up with interviewing, filing and writing letters to the guarantors. I can't say how many children were on my books, but it must have been in the thousands. Nor can I say how many I eventually got away, but it was only hundreds, alas.

Attention had primarily to be paid to the wishes of the guarantors. The majority stipulated girls of seven to ten and, if possible, fair. Boys of 12 and upwards were hard to place. Girls were in the majority on the transports. 'I tried to find the most urgent, helpless cases. This was not easy. Many were already refugees from Germany and Austria; many parents had "disappeared".'

Chadwick does not mention when exactly he took over as Honorary Secretary of the Children's Section of BCRC in Prague, but it must have been the beginning of March at the latest for, according to Warriner's report,

> On the 10th March, a special plane took my children from the YWCA to England, through Winton's organisation, by now in charge of Trevor Chadwick. Franz Brech I saw off with his parents on a transport; his face shone because he was going to Canada at last.

As this special 'plane' is not included in the official list, I can but guess that these were the children of the 'political' refugees, whose final destination was Canada.

After the occupation, it was impossible to organise the transports without official security; in all cases permission had to be granted by Kriminalrat Boemelberg, known to the Prague team as 'the criminal rat'. As head of the Gestapo, he was a man to be reckoned with and a man to be feared. Stopford and Warriner had to negotiate with him at every turn. He was particularly perplexed and furious that the huge group of Aryan Germans now in Prague could be anti-Nazi and would want to emigrate. He was responsible for the distribution of continuous propaganda, but few took the bait, despite the fact that the conditions under which they were living were appalling, the future uncertain and the longing for home strong. Boemelberg also played on the feelings of the wives whose husbands were already in Britain. Warriner describes how he addressed them personally:

> German women, you have parents, grandparents, graves in the Sudetenland. In the British Empire, dung for English fields, bought for £200 in exchange for your German birthright. If you return, I will give a letter of guarantee that no harm shall come to you.

When the women said they were determined to follow their men to England, the Kriminalrat insisted: 'Then promise to persuade your men to return.' To that a voice remarked dryly that the mayor of their Sudeten town had vowed that if her husband returned, he would execute him personally.

Chadwick saw another side of Boemelberg:

> The Nazis had arrived, but Kriminalrat Boemelberg was an elderly, smiling gentleman, far from sinister, who eventually proved to be a great help, sometimes unwittingly. He was really interested in my project and his only Nazi-ish remark was a polite query why England wanted so many Jewish children. He happily gave his stamp to the first train transport, even though I had included half a dozen 'adult' leaders on it. I went to the station accompanied by a Gestapo clerk, and all the children were there, with labels prepared by my helpers tied round their necks. The train took them off, cheering, through Germany to the Hook of Holland, a hundred or more.
>
> Soon Boemelberg sent for me. He said people were throwing dust in my eyes. It was now absolutely forbidden for any adult to leave the country without a special *Ausreisebewilligung* and the 'leaders' of my transport had really escaped illegally. I expressed my deepest sorrow and

grovelled. I was a blue-eyed boy again and thereafter he agreed to stamp my lists of children for transport without delay. I sealed my friendship with him by 'confessing' after the second transport that I had discovered later that one child was not Jewish. (There were several Aryans in all transports.) He praised my honesty and begged me to be careful, because of course the Nazis would look after 'Aryan' children.

Chadwick and Winton were not only concerned about the children in the protectorate. In Bratislava, the capital of Slovakia, refugees were dealt with by HICEM – an organisation that provided help for Jewish immigrants and emigrants. According to Winton's records, at the time Chadwick took over in Prague, there were 173 endangered children registered in Bratislava's HICEM office. It is interesting to note that 96 were refugees from Germany and the Sudetenland, 65 from Poland, Rumania and Hungary; only 12 were Slovak children. The conditions under which they existed were even worse than those of their fellow refugees in Prague, as Chadwick comments: 'While my Prague children were being vaguely fed by Jewish organisations, the Bratislava bunch's rations were rather dubious.' The two men made every effort to help this relatively small, distant group, as evident from the following letters, originally written in German:

Bratislava, 8 March 1939

Dear Mr Winton,

Your lovely letter of March 4th gave us great pleasure. From the information you sent and from your kind understanding, we can hope for the first time to free our children from their misery. Thank you for your dedication; may God repay you! As a result of your letter, we have sorted out 50 most urgent cases and these we have sent to Doreen Warriner at the Alcron Hotel.

Bratislava, 14 March 1939

Dear Mr Chadwick,

We acknowledge with deepest gratitude your kindness and helpful support which resulted in 12 of our children being taken to Prague, on their way to England. You yourself, Mr Chadwick, had personally witnessed the distress of these children, which turned into happiness for them and their parents. Please accept our warmest thanks. We beg you to continue helping us and understanding our situation.

I do not know how many children from Slovakia were eventually saved. Finding homes for them was far from easy. As Winton writes in his report of 31 July 1939: 'The Slovakian position is one which we have hardly started to tackle. The children are mostly orthodox and can only be placed in hostels. This we can arrange if funds are at our disposal.' In another report of the same date, Winton states:

> We have now selected from a registration total of 6,000 children, 400 urgent cases whom I consider should be dealt with by the Committee. Under this heading is included a scheme arranged by Youth Aliyah to bring over 200 children, for which they naturally need financial aid. Most of these children would be re-emigrated to Palestine, but some would remain for agricultural work in England. Further, included in the above, are urgent cases in Slovakia for whom, up to the present, we have been unable to do anything whatsoever.

With 6,000 children still on their books, only one more transport was to leave, on 2 August, with 68 children. How heartbreaking it must have been for Winton, Chadwick and all concerned that so many were left behind, most of them to perish. If only there had been less red tape, more time, more funds, more help from other countries! Winton had pinned his hopes on America opening her doors and offering refuge. He wrote to every conceivable office he could think of, pleading for help, pointing out the danger and the urgency of the situation. Sadly, his efforts came to nothing. Vague promises were made, but left unfulfilled; hopes were raised, then crushed.

The following three replies are to be found in the scrapbook:

26 May 1939

Dear Mr Winton,

I wish to thank you for your letter. I have placed it in the hands of a Committee which is trying to arrange to include Czechoslovakian children within the provisions of the Wagner–Rogers Bill. This latter would make possible the bringing over of 10,000 children per year for each of two years out of Germany to America, these outside of the quota.

Faithfully yours,
Dr Stephen S. Wise,
President, American Jewish Congress,
New York City.

27 May 1939

My dear Mr Winton,

I was glad to have your letter of May 16th regarding children from Czechoslovakia. The children refugee bill recently approved by a joint sub-committee of the House and Senate specifically includes children from Czechoslovakia. The bill, as you may know, provides for the admission within the next two years of 20,000 German refugee children outside the quota. I am very hopeful that it will be enacted at the present session of Congress.

Very sincerely yours,
Robert F. Wagner,
United States Senator, Washington DC.

7 June 1939

Dear Sir,

I desire to acknowledge the receipt of your letter of May 16, 1939, addressed to the President of the United States on the subject of refugee children of Czechoslovakia. I also beg leave to state in reply that the United States Government is unable, in the absence of specific legislation, to permit immigration in excess of that provided for by existing immigration laws. However, in view of the possibility that private organizations might be in a position to be of some assistance, a copy of your letter was forwarded to the President's Advisory Committee on Political Refugees in New York City.

Very truly yours,
Robert E. Schoenfeld,
First Secretary of Embassy,
American Embassy,
London.

How could they have not realised, after receiving Winton's explicit letters, that by postponing or avoiding the issue they were sealing the children's fate? To this day, Winton finds it difficult to understand and forgive their attitude.

Yet this laid-back attitude was shared by many, even in Britain. The Home Office, as Winton had pointed out earlier, were slow in sending documents, which added to Chadwick's frustrations:

They just didn't realise. If only the Home Secretary could have spent a few days with me, seeing brutality, listening to, not arguing with, young Nazis, as I often did, he would doubtlessly have pushed the whole thing along fast. If he had realised that the regulations were for so many children the first nudge along the wretched road to Auschwitz, he would, of course, have immediately imported the lot. But that is too much wisdom after the event.

It is obvious that Chadwick was doing an excellent job, as confirmed by both Doreen Warriner and Winton, but London gradually became uneasy about his association with Boemelberg. Chadwick did not keep it a secret and, at first, no one had any objections; it proved most useful in speeding up the process of getting the children away. As on occasions Chadwick participated in helping the political refugees escape and was witness to the cruel methods the Gestapo used and the terror they caused, it seems unlikely and out of character that he would fall prey to the Kriminalrat's propaganda and assurances that Aryan children and their parents, whatever their allegiances, would be safe and better off back in their homeland. Although Doreen Warriner says in her account that the Nazis suspected in him a potential convert and he lead them on, as time went on the situation became more complex and it seemed advisable from all sides for Chadwick to return to Britain. On this subject he ends his account:

> Boemelberg remained friendly and things were going as smoothly as possible, but in the evenings there were other fish to fry which did not have anything to do with the children. It became obvious to me as summer developed that certain of my movements were at least suspect and that B. and his boys might turn sour. This would jeopardize the children, so I explained these things to London and they arranged a replacement. I shall always have a feeling of shame that I didn't get more out.

The exact date of Chadwick's departure is not known. From documents available we know that he was still in Prague on 26 June 1939. Mr T.R.M. Creighton then became honorary secretary of the Children's Section, but I have been unable to glean any information about him.

There is no doubt that without Winton's success in finding guarantors and foster homes for the children only a fraction of those who were saved would have escaped. Yet, with two exceptions, all these years we, the Winton children, have lived in ignorance of his existence and his deed – that is until 1988. The two refugees who met him did not do so until after the onset of war, at his mother's house. By then, his frantic days in Prague and equally frantic occasions on meeting the trains at Liverpool Street Station were hardly suitable for introductions. Chadwick was more involved with the children during his time in Prague and he is remembered fondly by many of them.

Margit Friedmann (now Fazakerley) met him as an eight-year-old. 'He touched me with his kindness', she says. 'How can one forget a man who picked me up, put me on his lap, wiped away my tears and comforted me?' She recalls a room in Prague crammed with other refugee children and 'her' Chadwick teaching them to sing *Baa Baa Black Sheep*. Margit's mother told her that he would take her to England, but he failed to join her transport and she was panic-stricken, one question only on her mind: 'How will Mummy find me again when Chadwick isn't with me?' That first night at her foster home, she wanted to beg not to be left alone, but did not know the words. 'I put my arms round my foster mother's neck – she pulled them away. If she had hugged me, I would have opened up like a flower.' Weeks later, she heard the infant class of her school singing *Baa Baa Black Sheep*. She burst through the door, fully expecting to see her hero, but there was no Chadwick. She never saw him, her parents, or her little sister again.

Henry Schermer, who left Prague on a *kindertransport* on 11 May, remembers a fleeting meeting with Chadwick when the validity of his travel document was questioned. As he tried to converse in his pidgin English, Chadwick burst into merry laughter at the lad's misuse of words and thus alleviated a tense situation. (Harry's cousin, Ruth Reser, was one of the two 'young helpers' in Chadwick's office.)

Ingeborg Wohlmann (now Pedelty), originally from Vienna, met Chadwick when she and her sister (aged nine and six) were taken by their mother for an interview.

My memory is of a smiling man who put my very nervous mother at ease. At one point, he mimed that he needed the help of a big book, but pulled out the smallest book I had ever seen – it must have been a dictionary. He made us all laugh. We left on the last plane.

101

The two boys Chadwick brought out of Prague to his home and school were not the only youngsters taken in by the family. Eleven-year-old Gerda Stein (now Gerda Mayer, the poet) had fled to Prague from Karlsbaad, in the Sudetenland, with her parents and 18-year-old sister. Her parents, desperate to emigrate, spent all their time rushing fruitlessly from office to office, consulate to consulate. Everywhere the answer was negative; there was no hope; even the *kindertransports* were full up. Gerda's father, determined to have one last try, managed to find out the name of the hotel in which Chadwick was staying. To his relief and delight, Chadwick accepted Gerda at once. What is more, he took her to live in his own home and made his mother her guarantor. Gerda still has vivid recollections of their meeting:

> It took place in the Alcron, Prague's best hotel. We had all dressed very neatly for the occasion, my father in a formal suit. Trevor Chadwick, tall, handsome, with strikingly Nordic looks, descended the stairs, dressed in an old fisherman's jersey!

And in her diary, an entry on 22 February 1939 reads: 'He is terribly charming. Perhaps I'll go to his house on the English Riviera through the Anglican Church. It will be wonderful there.'

Gerda's sister was too old to be included in the transports; she survived, but her parents perished.

Chadwick returned to his family only briefly. After he was called up, his sons did not see him for 11 years. After his first wife divorced him, he married a second time, but his new, domineering wife insisted he sever all links with his former family, threatening suicide at the mere mention of their names. Needless to say, the marriage was doomed to failure.

His wartime years were eventful and varied. He joined the coastal command as an ordinary seaman, then the Royal Air Force Volunteer Reserve attaining the rank of Flying Officer. In September 1941 he was court-martialled for failing to report for duty for two weeks 'until apprehended by civil powers'. No doubt it was his charm and ability to talk his way out of any situation that secured him a light sentence. He was obviously immensely efficient in his job which included dealing with the families and effects of airmen killed in action. Although demoted to Pilot Officer for this offence, he regained his rank within eight months and soon after reached the rank of Flight Lieutenant. His wartime activities ended in 1943 when he was invalided out of the Force after suffering an injury in a jeep accident in North Africa.

By 1951 the years of hard living had taken their toll. His health was broken and he was critically ill with tuberculosis. It was five years before he was back to reasonable health. He settled in Oslo where he established, together with friends, the Oslo University Press. Nine years later he met his third wife, Sigi, to whom he was happily married for the rest of his life. He died on 23 December 1979, the same year as Doreen Warriner.

Sigi, who has lived in England since Chadwick's retirement in 1975, regrets very much that he did not live to meet at least some of the children since he often wondered what had become of them.

Dorothea Douglas (née Koniecova) was one of the few Slovak children saved and also recalls Chadwick's small office where she and her brother, Herbert, registered. Dorothea is the only former refugee, that I know of, to contact Chadwick after the publication of his article in Karen Gershon's book. In his reply to her (1966) from Oslo, he wrote:

> Except for letters from my mother mentioning a Jewish girl (Gerda Mayer) this is my first contact with one of 'my children' from Czechoslovakia. Of course, I don't count the two boys adopted by our school. I wish I could remember you all …

* * *

When Doreen Warriner opened the BCRC office in Prague in October 1938 to deal with the many thousands of refugees, she desperately needed help and Bill Barazetti was assigned to her as secretary. This 24-year-old non-Jewish man had left his native Switzerland early in that year to avoid further embarrassment to his father's brother who was a high-ranking army oficer, whereas Barazetti was well known for his anti-Nazi feelings and activities. He had always looked upon Prague almost as the capital of his second homeland, but then his family's history and his own life were closely interwoven with the Czech lands.

Long before he was born, when Bohemia and Moravia were part of the Austro-Hungarian Empire under the Emperor Franz Josef, Barazetti's grandfather, Le Monnier, was the Chief of Police in Brno (the capital of Moravia). Le Monnier's son and daughter needed to learn Czech as new regulations at their school stipulated that all examinations had to be conducted in Czech as well as German. Help came from an unexpected quarter. 'I was top of the class and was therefore recommended as a tutor to the family of the Chief of Police. Le Monnier was about the grandest man in Brno', explains Tomas Masaryk, in *Discussions with T.G. Masaryk* by Karel Capek. Masaryk became the founder president of the Czechoslovak Republic in 1918, but back in 1865 he was a poor teenager in his second year at a Brno gymnasium. 'They fed me every day so well that I also managed to look after my brother during his studies. Later on, the chief was transferred to Vienna and he took me along.'

In Vienna, Masaryk attended university and lived with the family. By then Le Monnier had been promoted to the position of President of the Imperial Police. His son Franz and Masaryk remained close friends throughout their student years and later political upheavals. One professor, who did not much care for Masaryk or Franz, shouted at them: 'You two will never get anywhere in life, you are just a nuisance!' Some years later, the same professor had to go to the Ministry of Education in Vienna regarding his salary, only to find that Franz was the ministerial counsellor to whom he had to plead his case. It is to be hoped that the professor was still alive when Masaryk became president.

Barazetti lived with his Czech wife Anna in Hornchurch, in Essex, until his death in 2000. When Muriel and I interviewed him in 1996, he recalled with pleasure the occasions when, as a small boy, he had met Masaryk and then went on to tell us more about his life.

He spent his childhood in Zurich and in 1933 he went to university to study philosophy and economics, first in Prague then in Hamburg. It was in Hamburg where he first became aware of the rising anti-Jewish movement. After witnessing the dreadful treatment, the arrests and even murder of Jewish and Communist students by Hitler's mobs, he returned to Prague and implored his Jewish friends to get out while they could. An ardent anti-Nazi, he readily agreed to work for the Czech Intelligence, who asked him to spy for them in Germany, using his family connections and personal contacts to try to find out what Hitler's future plans might be. Barazetti unhesitatingly complied and set up a perfume factory as a cover for his clandestine activities. When in the autumn of 1936 the suspicions of the Germans were aroused, he faked his own death and fled to Poland, changing his appearance and identity before returning to Germany to carry on with his clandestine activities. Eventually he was caught on the Czech–German border by the Gestapo, beaten up and left for dead. A young peasant woman found him and nursed him back to health; this was Anna, who became his wife. Soon afterwards they returned to Prague, Barazetti on a forged passport with the name of his great-grandfather Le Monnier.

With such a background, coupled with further cloak and dagger adventures, it was hardly surprising that Barazetti volunteered to join the BCRC. His main job originally was to smooth the way with government administration and to ensure that no Nazi spies had a free passage to England when groups of refugees and other enemies of the Reich began to leave. Doreen Warriner had been desperate to find someone she could trust as Prague was riddled with spies.

'I used to know most of them', Barazetti told me. 'Big Nazis, small crooks and their innocent victims.' He continued to work under the assumed name of Le Monnier because he was afraid of endangering the rescue operation if his past anti-Nazi activities came to light.

105

Winton describes his first meeting with Barazetti in a letter to his mother sent from Prague in January 1939:

> At 1 o'clock I went to Barazetti (the secretary of Miss Warriner) to fetch him for lunch and then the real rush started. I need hardly say that we never got to lunch and that our first meal was at 9.30 in the evening.
>
> All the people who want to see Miss Warriner for information or help are asked to go any or every day to Vorsilska 2. There they are met by Barazetti (and today me as well) and they are dealt with ...
>
> Questions about how to get to England, as though it only needed a magic carpet which, by the way, is about what it does need at the moment, questions about parents being willing to pay something towards their children's upkeep in England if we could only expedite the emigration. Actually it is now practically impossible to get the National Bank to grant foreign exchange for anything. Mothers who wanted to get their children to England but would not be parted from them. Could we find someone in England who would take both child and mother?'

Before leaving Prague in January 1939, Winton asked Barazetti to be 'the responsible official for all children in Czechoslovakia who wish to come to England' – a position he held until Chadwick's arrival at the beginning of March.

As Warriner's secretary, Barazetti was primarily involved in helping endangered adults to reach safer havens, but for thousands there was no escape. He was then faced with the all too familiar pleas: 'If you can't help us, can you please at least save our children?' Thus, he too played a vital part in the rescue of the little ones throughout his stay in Prague. Sometime after 2 August 1939, when the eighth transport left Prague with 68 children, he reluctantly returned to Switzerland from where he made his way to Britain. He felt that war had become unavoidable and was anxious to do his bit for the war effort.

For five years Barazetti worked for the British Secret Service, interrogating German prisoners of war, mainly the crews of sunken boats or submarines and German airmen whose planes had been shot down. His ties with Czechoslovakia remained strong throughout his life.

For 20 years Barazetti, by now a British citizen, was the International Honorary Treasurer of PEN (a pressure group campaigning, *inter alia*, on behalf of imprisoned writers). He made Britain his home, after fleeing from Prague, where he lived until his death, together with his wife and four children.

As a gentile, with no Jewish ancestors, who was exposed to danger under the Nazis whilst helping to save lives, Barazetti was awarded the honour of Righteous Gentile, by Yad Vashem in Israel. This ceremony took place on 31 October 1993 in the presence of about 100 people, including the Czech ambassador and 25 men and women who, as children, had left Prague on the *kindertransports*. Moving tributes were paid both to Barazetti and Winton by two of the former refugees who, like so many others, will always remain indebted to them.

In his speech, Hugo Maron (formerly Meisl) expresses his gratitude on behalf of us all:

> I stand here and now to pay tribute from the bottom of my heart on behalf of all those present, the missing majority of lucky children and their parents, wherever they may be on earth or in heaven, to thank Bill Barazetti, Nicholas Winton and all their companions, living or dead, who I hope can also hear our thanks from this sacred place. Saving a single Jew from Nazi jaws deserved this, Israel's highest and only offical recognition. All that we, who were saved by Bill Barazetti, can say is thank you! How can two simple words like 'thank you' cover this selfless, audacious and courageous work, which saved not one, but hundreds of children's lives?

Tom Berman closed his speech with the following words:

> On behalf of the Czech *kinder*, on behalf of our parents and families who did not survive; with reverence, awe and humility I ask Bill Barazetti to unveil this plaque which

honours him and is a token of our gratitude and a symbol of Light which he gave us in days of Darkness.

* * *

During the months between the annexation of the Sudetenland and the German occupation, quite a number of foreign volunteers came to Prague to join the loosely connected team under Doreen Warriner; they were all anxious to get as many endangered people to safety as possible. Prague was full of German spies at that time and great care had to be taken that no German spy could use the exodus of refugees as a means of slipping unobtrusively into Britain. Czech officials and British diplomats warned repeatedly of such a possibility. Once their suspicions were aroused, the volunteers checked everyone most carefully and soon discovered that such warnings were fully justified and that some of the tales of woe related by the so-called enemies of the Third Reich were completely fabricated. Bill Barazetti must have played an important part in locating such impostors. After all, that was his main job, and his forte! Thus, fortunately, not many – if any – Nazi spies reached Britain as part of a group of genuine refugees.

The Society of Friends (the Quakers) were well aware during the years preceeding the war of the growing threat of fascism. From their offices in major cities of Germany and Austria they monitored with concern the constantly escalating persecution of Jews. Quakers have a tradition of ministering to refugees; it is therefore no wonder that they were actively involved in bringing out several groups of adults and children from Germany and helping in the escape and with the upkeep of many more. Five or six of their members were sent to Prague to help with relief work and emigration.

Some members preferred to act independently. Jean Hoare, a cousin of the then Home Secretary, Sir Samuel Hoare (who came from a Quaker family), flew to Prague just before the occupation, armed with donations from the RIBA (Royal Institute of British Architects) and returned with 46 children in

108

tow. Jean Bannister was another member of the Society of
Friends. Winton remembers her as a beautiful 28-year-old who
worked tirelessly for children and adults in Prague and in
Bratislava. Tessa Rowntree, also a Quaker, escorted several
groups fleeing through Poland or Germany, often enduring
harrassment and questioning by the Gestapo.

The March invasion took Tessa and the others completely by
surprise. 'It seems criminal that those of us working for refugees
in Prague were not given a little notice, as we might have packed
off hundreds of refugees whose emigration plans were almost or
quite completed', she wrote to the editor of the American
journal *Friend*. 'Now they are in concentration camps, or have
committeed suicide, or have gone illegally to Poland.' Tessa
failed to mention in her letter that after 15 March she spent
much time with fellow workers stuffing papers and passports
down the toilets in their hotel. 'We felt that had the Nazis found
the passports and the owners, that would have been the end for
many of the latter.'

Now that the country was in German hands, British
diplomats urged all British volunteers to leave immediately.
Some acted on that advice, others remained. As already
mentioned, Doreen Warriner had to leave six weeks after the
invasion to avoid internment.

Tessa Rowntree wanted to remain in the protectorate, but
after constant warnings from British diplomats she felt she must
leave, and with reluctance returned to Britain. She visited
Prague after the war and discovered that some of the Czech
Quakers with whom she had worked in 1939, and who had
become close friends, had perished in Nazi concentration
camps. This shows only too clearly that the volunteer workers
were, to some extent, exposed to danger.

Quite a few Winton children went to Quaker families or were
funded by them. My own Methodist foster family heard of
Winton's rescue mission through the society, which worked
closely with other Jewish and Christian agencies. Quakers were
always ready to help in any way they could. For instance,
members were invited to guarantee the cost of individual
maintenance, or re-emigration. This appealed more to donors

than making an impersonal contribution, and often resulted in a lasting friendship being forged between donor and child.

Karel Reisz, the well-known film director, is an excellent example. The youngest son of a Czech-Jewish solicitor and his Sudeten-German wife, Reisz owes his life not only to Winton, but also to the Quakers. A couple of years prior to the war, his parents, sensing trouble in the air, sent his older brother Paul to a Quaker boarding school in Reading, supposedly to learn English. (They chose the Quaker school as it was more liberal than most.) After the German occupation Paul asked the head if he would accept his brother too. This he did, and must have waived the fees for both boys. Karel says that

> Quakers are amazingly generous-spirited. They found a lady in Reading, a Miss Stanfield, to put down the necessary £50 and to be my guarantor. I remember visiting her regularly for tea. I was extraordinarily fortunate. On arrival, the head took me into his study. He spoke a little German and I a little English. I was 13 years old and dressed in shorts and knee-length socks, held by an elastic band. The head joked about this, then said, 'I know what you need, young man – a bicycle', and he drove me in his Rover into the centre of the town and bought one for me! I rode it proudly, following his Rover, back to the school. I spent the following four years there.

Another outstanding individual was German-born, non-Jewish Greta Burkill, the somewhat unconventional daughter of a left-wing journalist, who was married to a Cambridge don. An ardent anti-fascist, she threw herself into refugee work and set up, in her Quaker home, the Cambridge Refugee Committee. Similarly to Jean Hoare, Greta brought to Britain a large group of refugee children, but from Germany. She took a keen interest in their education and in the education of child refugees of all nationalities. She excelled at persuading private schools in the area to accept the children at reduced fees – or no fees at all – and somehow always managed to find finances for their degree courses. If a child happened to be academically gifted, Gerda

Burkill did everything in her power to give him or her the best possible education.

Susanne Medas, who came to Britain with the Woodcraft Folk, found her most helpful. Susanne was only just young enough to be included in the *kindertransport* and therefore, soon after her arrival in England, was old enough to earn her own living. Her guarantor was the Cambridge Refugee Committee and Greta Burkill wanted her to have a university education. Susanne told me:

> I turned down her generous offer, but I was glad to accept help to get into teachers' training college; I wanted and needed to earn my living. The Cambridge Committee took good care of us. Mrs Greta Burkill, with her friendly and always cheerful welcome in her large house, her three children and a variety of animals of all kinds and sizes, is someone I shall never forget.

It is due mainly to Greta Burkill that Cambridge soon became one of the most active and largest centres for young refugees.

* * *

Only recently I had the privilege to meet a remarkable woman – Josephine Pike. Wheelchair-bound and very frail, she could barely speak, but was able to recall, with the help of her devoted husband, the turbulent months in 1939 she had spent in and around Prague. Josephine, then Read, was still in her teens when she responded to the stories of the hardships refugees were suffering in the protectorate. Her genuine love of children prompted her to go at her own expense, without any plans, to see what she could do to help. A convent-educated linguist, she persuaded the Convent of Saint Clothilde to let her have a small room where she proceeded to feed, clothe and educate as many deprived children as she could cram into her room. (Most of the refugee children were not allowed to attend Czech schools; many could not speak the language.) Most importantly, she brought a little happiness and laughter and some order and stability into the children's drab, insecure lives. She filled their days with lessons and song and taught them to love nature, to plant seeds and flowers and watch them grow. Once or twice during her stay she escorted several children to England, where she persuaded British children to buy sweets and little presents for them with their pocket money to take back for the not so fortunate youngsters left behind.

Some of her charges left on the *kindertransports*. She was always there, on the station platform, to see them off. She was one of the few who refused to leave after the occupation, wanting to protect and care for those who had no hope of getting to safety. Yet at times she was exposed to danger and scared out of her mind. Josephine still recoils from the memory of an incident when two excited youngsters – brother and sister – accompanied by their parents led her to their patch of land where potato shoots had just burst through the soil. For some unknown reason, a German soldier appeared and shot both the parents and then the protesting children.

I did not hear of Josephine until April 1998. A couple of months later, the Czech Embassy in London were giving a reception to some of the former refugee children and those who helped to save them. On my request, Josephine and her husband David were invited. Knowing how frail she was, I never dreamt they would make the long journey from their home on the Isle of Man. To my amazement and delight, they did make it and I was happy and proud to acknowledge publicly the role she had played and to thank her for making the lives of the children she took under her care worth living.

Her husband wrote on their return home:

> We are deeply indebted to you for the welcome at the Embassy. Jo feels that at last she has returned home. In spite of the dangers and conditions in 1939, it was one of the happiest times of her life.

Sadly, soon after our meeting, Josephine passed away.

* * *

The Christadelphians faith is based on Jewish law. They were very involved in running the hostels and finding homes for child refugees. Alan Overton, a shopkeeper, living on the out skirts of Rugby, was an incredibly active, concerned member. He had always had a keen interest in the Jewish people and had watched with excitement their gradual return to Palestine. The developments taking place there from 1918 led him to speak on the subject at public meetings and attend debates in the House of Commons until 1948, when the State of Israel was declared.

The publicity surrounding the arrival of the first *kindertransport* from Germany made him aware of the extreme need and urgency of the situation as it was towards the end of 1938. His son Bruce has vivid recollections of that occasion:

> I remember, although I was only ten years old at the time, a photograph of a little girl, her hair in plaits, sitting forlornly on the platform of the station, her backpack at her side, a label tied round her neck. My father was so moved, for he had three young daughters of his own, that from then on he was determined to do all he could for these sorrowful refugee children. He placed advertisements in and wrote articles for the *Christadelphian Magazine* appealing for helpers, and everywhere he spoke and lectured he continued to appeal for homes and sponsors for the children.
>
> Our home became virtually a transit house. Often late at night, my father would arrive after meeting the boat train in London, his car packed with children, some feeling very unwell after the long journey, besides the trauma of leaving their parents. How my mother coped, with her own four children plus the house full to overflowing, I shall never know.

As the Nazi threat to the Jews grew in intensity and the fear of hostilities increased, Alan Overton, with a circle of supporters, lobbied and pleaded with members of parliament not to close the doors of Britain to those seeking refuge and asylum, particularly to the children. Like Winton, he was determined to help save as many as possible. He soon realised that there was a dire need for a hostel to be set up in Rugby as a permanent home for boys. Most foster-parents preferred to take girls and they were placed more easily in families in and around Rugby and elsewhere. Many German refugee boys and some Winton children were given refuge in Christadelphian homes and hostels and there is substantial documentation to show how closely Overton worked with Winton and, later, with Winton's mother, who took over the care of the children once war started. I do not think he ever turned a child away.

One of the boys needing help was Hanus Snabl, who arrived in Britain on the transport with me on 1 July 1939. He spent the first year with a teacher's family in Essex; they were so kind that they even turned their own son out of his bedroom so that Hanus would have a proper bed in which to sleep. When his benefactor joined the Navy, there was no money to spare. Hanus then went to the hostel for refugee boys near Rugby.

Many years later, when Hanus visited Alan Overton, he brought down from the loft his proudest possession – an old cardboard box, with more than two hundred labels – the name tags that the children wore round their necks when they came into his care; each label represented a life he had helped to save.

Bruce Overton ends the recollections of his father, so aptly, so movingly:

> Many years have now passed since those days. Most of the people who worked so hard during those sad and gruelling times have passed away. But the children whose lives were literally saved from certain death are now in their sixties and seventies. Some have thought back to the days when, on arrival in England, in a free, but strange land, they were met by a young man who comforted and cheered them and became a 'father' to them. A father I, for one, was proud to share.

* * *

The Woodcraft Folk (Red Falcons) are an international youth movement with strong socialist leanings. Some time ago I had the pleasure of meeting their former National Organiser at a gathering of people whose lives he had helped to save. Henry Fair, known to all members as Koodoo, died in Somerset in February 1999 at the age of 91. He had helped to save the lives of about 20 Czech children, a role for which he is remembered and loved to this day. A year after organising an international camp in Brighton in 1937, he was alerted to the danger that many children living in the occupied territories were facing as members of a socialist youth organisation, as well as those who were Jewish. This caused him to circulate to all Woodcraft groups the following letter:

THE WOODCRAFT FOLK
13 Ritherdon Road
Tooting, London, SW17.

Circular from National Organiser

1st November 1938

Greetings, Comrades,

Last week I had a visitor from Prague, a friend of Willi Hocke's, whom most of you remember as the leader of the Czech delegation at the International Camp (1937).

She came, not on a sightseeing tour of London, but on an urgent mission of help for the Red Falcons of Czechoslovakia. In July, the Red Falcons held a camp of several hundreds at Bodenbach which was on the Czech–German frontier. Willi writes to me this week to say that there are now only five groups left inside the new Czech frontiers.

What of the others? Both the girl tells me and Willi writes to me that hundreds of the parents of Red Falcon members are in peril of their lives, hundreds are refugees, sleeping in fields and ditches. Their children, ex Red Falcons, many of them came to Brighton, are amongst these and they plead with their fellow comrades of other countries for help. Well, what can we do, what can you do?

Firstly, Willi is organising the emigration of some hundreds to Belgium which will allow them entry. This needs money and you can help with this. Secondly, there is every possibility of some coming to England providing we can give them hospitality for a few months whilst arrangements are made for their future. The Society of Friends are willing to take up any offers of help from Folk members especially where accommodation and hospitality can be given and they will explore the question of education for such children.

Now, comrades, here is our chance to show our solidarity with our Czech comrades. Can you take a boy or girl or perhaps two boys or girls? Talk this over immediately, ask for copies of this circular for giving to Pioneers' parents.

If accommodation cannot be offered, then send a donation to the above address for passing on to Willi, get your children to collect their pennies and help with this. I know that the Folk's own financial position is precarious and we need cash ourselves, but this is a period of sacrifice by the workers for the workers. London Kin took a collection last Sunday at the Unity Theatre and raised £4.0.6 as a kick off. Who's going to beat this?

Friendship and Solidarity,
Koodoo, National Organiser.

The letter had the desired effect. In fact, more homes were found in Britain among the Woodcraft Folk than children to fill them. They travelled to England in one small group, together with their leader, Vikki Schless, in July 1939. Most of them were in their teens. They were part of a large *kindertransport* from Prague, which had been organised by Nicky Winton, who also helped to raise the £50 per head required by the British government to guarantee their re-emigration.

Sue Pearson, who was one of the younger girls, recalls:

I well remember Koodoo meeting us, a bewildered little group, at Liverpool Street Station. His broad and winning smile – which remained with him to the end of his life – and his pure cockney voice were reassuring, even if not always understood by us.

116

Koodoo translated his beliefs into the way he lived. A socialist, internationalist and pacifist, he clearly loved people and children in particular. His 50-year service to the Labour Party was rewarded by Neil Kinnock at a National Conference in 1984. His lifetime work was devoted to youth and education.

Several of us remained in touch with him and when in 1991 he joined us in a reunion of old Red Falcons in Prague, we were glad to have the oppportunity to express our gratitude publicly for the part he had played in our survival.

Susanne Medas, who, back in 1939, was one of the older girls, has vivid recollections of that landmark in their lives:

Leaving our families wasn't all that traumatic for us older ones. Most of us knew each other; it seemed like going on another holiday. The highlight of our journey was our reception at the Dutch border, where we were welcomed with hot cocoa and cakes and people cheering. I was nearly 16 years old when I arrived at Liverpool Street Station, along with a full trainload of mostly younger children. We were led into a large and gloomy shed and there the 'distribution' took place. The members of my group were met by Koodoo who took them, together with Vikki Schless, to a camp in Essex for the first week, from where they sent a postcard to Winton and his mother, thanking them for their help. I had been found a home in Cambridge by my elder brother, who had reached England via France some weeks earlier. Those of us who were travelling to the provinces had labels round our necks, rather like big parcels; mine said 'CAMBRIDGE' and I was taken there by a young American girl, who could speak German.

Now I know that both Nicky Winton and his mother met that particular transport. How I wish I had known of his existence at the time! Perhaps I had passed him on the platform, perhaps it was he who called out the names of the children for whom

117

guarantors were waiting, in that large gloomy hall. Like Susanne I had a label round my neck, mine with 'LIVERPOOL' written on it, but unlike all the other children, including my sister, I was left sitting there, all alone. No one came to claim me. I was seized with such panic, I have never been so terrified. Was it perhaps Winton who personally arranged for me to be taken to some bishop's residence, where I stayed for two or three days until my foster mother was able to come to fetch me? He cannot remember, so we shall never know!

Winton has vivid recollections of other incidents of that day:

> Looking back on it now, I really don't quite know how we managed to sort out the chaos which ensued when the train pulled in. I remember someone standing on a pile of luggage and shouting out the name of a child and then the name of a guarantor. When they got together, we obtained a signature and shouted out the next name. To add to the difficulties, some of the guarantors were orthodox Jews, who would neither carry luggage, nor sign for the children because, as luck would have it, July 1st was a Saturday. But the children were safe in England and all these problems were just minor irritations.

According to Winton, his mother soon solved that particular problem. Never the one to mince her words, she marched up to those who refused to co-operate on religious grounds and said 'My son has worked day and night and done everything possible to save these children and you say that you can't break the Jewish law. What sort of nonsense is that?' Tall and stately, she cut a somewhat formidable figure, matched by her powerful voice. There were no further objections. The children were duly signed for, the luggage was picked up and all was well.

Barbara Winton played a very active part in her son's rescue mission, in fact she met every single transport and almost ran the office single-handed when war started and Winton was no longer available. She took a special interest in the Red Falcon group from Prague. Vikki Schless, who now lives in Germany, recalls that during his stay in London in 1939 and 1940, he never met Winton, but got to know his mother quite well. 'My visits to dear Mrs Winton meant a great deal to me', he told me. 'She felt great sympathy for us, the refugees from the leftist camp; she always appeared to be such a kind, mother figure, and as such she remains in my memory to this day.'

This sentiment was echoed by the late Ruth Bratu, one of the Red Falcon group. She wrote:

> I was only 15 years old when I left and I never knew of Winton's role in our rescue, though I visited his mother in her lovely flat in Baker Street many times during the war. She was a warm-hearted motherly friend to me and always ready with helpful advice. It was Mrs Winton who helped me to get my first job – in her brother's factory for surgical equipment.

Susanne Medas also has fond memories of Barbara Winton and is one of the very few who at that time actually also met her son:

> It was during the early war years, when Londoners were losing their homes during the heavy raids, that the Americans sent a lot of secondhand clothing to be distributed among the victims. Barbara Winton heard about this and promptly contacted the organisers to make sure that some of these clothes could go to 'her' refugee children who, by then, had long since outgrown what they had brought from home.
>
> So my first encounter with her was in London, where the basement of a large store was fitted out with rails and shelves and was stacked with jackets and coats, sweaters and shoes, all in excellent condition. But my own memory is not so much of the lovely jacket which I wore many years until the lining disintegrated, but of my first encounter with this tall, elegant lady, as she stood on the kerb, a fox-fur round her shoulders, her hand raised with a majestic air, to stop a taxi. I was deeply impressed! I remember her as a firm, sensible woman who did not suffer fools gladly

and who had a grip on life that was reassuring. I had not met such a person before.

Susanne did not meet Winton until the war ended, when she was visiting his mother. 'I fell in love with him at once', she says. 'He looked so handsome in his uniform. I am glad to say I never spoke about my feelings – somehow I don't think that Mrs Winton would have liked to know that I harboured such thoughts.'

I have come across several letters, written in German and included in the scrapbook, which show that both Winton and his mother were also helping to reunite families of political and Jewish refugees who had initially fled to Prague from the Sudetenland:

Boulogne, 2 May 1939

Dear Mr Winton,

We, the undersigned, received the news yesterday that our wives and children have arrived safely in England and we felt it right to convey to you our heartfelt thanks. We will be eternally grateful.

The letter is signed by 16 men. This proves that it helped to split families to get them to safety, as does the following letter from a grateful mother already in London:

London, 6 June 1939

Dear Mrs Winton,

Thank you for your valuable help in making it possible for me to have my little Eva with me once more. Thank you for all you did and all the trouble you went to to bring my little one to me.

Signed (Mitzi Pfeifer)

One of the most touching letters in the scrapbook is addressed again to Mrs Winton:

Prague, 15 August 1939

Dear Mrs Winton,

I got your address from my brother-in-law, Mr Henry Frank. He informed me that you especially greatly helped him to find a new home for our son, Tommy Frank. We know very well how much trouble you, dear Mrs Winton, must have gone to. I thank you with all my heart for your help. Thousands of parents from our country thank you with all their heart as we do, thousands wait for news from you and from Bloomsbury House, as we did. May God bless you and your assistants, Mr Lewinsohn and Mr Klaus, for all your trouble, your love, your work and your help. We will never forget what you did for us and for what you will do for other children.

Sincerely yours, Martha Frank.

Tommy Frank's name is on the list of the children brought over – his first destination, a hostel in Edmonton Castle, near Carlisle; his guarantor a Rosina Philp from Clacton-on-Sea; and the guarantor for the re-emigration liability was the Czech Section (Czech Refugee Trust Fund). This plainly illustrates the frequent difficulties in finding homes and funds to satisfy the Home Office before permits were granted.

Susanne kept in touch with Mrs Winton throughout the years. She says:

My last memories of her are sad ones. She was then over 90 and had chosen to live in a home for the elderly, which in itself must have been a severe blow to her pride and independence. I visited her there several times. I was too inexperienced to know about senile dementia and also how people can change when of necessity all decision-making has been taken away from them. But I am glad that I kept in contact and that, just by visiting her, I could bring back to her those early years when she freely gave her time to the aftercare of the children whose lives had been saved by her son.

121

Susanne Medas, formerly Bernstein, was born in Berlin and emigrated to Prague in 1933 from where she came to England on a Winton transport. Like most of Winton's children she never saw her parents again. She now divides her time between Britain and the Czech Republic.

As far as I know, and I am in contact with about 250 of the Winton children, Susanne is the only one who actually met him at that turbulent time and even then it was at the very end of the war. He did not discuss what he had accomplished and neither did his mother. Far from boasting, he kept very much in the background, even in those days.

Koodoo recalled that in 1939 he did not deal with Winton's office directly, but through the Society of Friends, who often acted as intermediaries and were always there to help. In the Woodcraft Folk case, most of the offers of homes came from relatively poor families and extra funding had to be found, not just for the guarantees, but also for everyday needs and help with the children's education, as some of the foster families could not shoulder the responsibility alone. Koodoo turned to the Quakers many times.

Although aware of Winton's existence, he did not meet him personally until 1993 when the three of us attended a gathering of the former Red Falcon 'children' to which we had been invited. There was no doubt in Koodoo's mind that those present could not have escaped without Winton's efforts.

NO TIME TO SAY GOODBYE

I have in my possession a long list of names – supposedly of all the children who came on the *kindertransports* from Prague, with dates of birth, their sponsors, guarantors and destinations in Britain. Discrepancies in the list are explained in the Appendix.

Whilst I do not doubt the accuracy of the list – it is a sacred list, for each entry represents a life saved by Winton – the scrapbook also provides an authentic record of what went on during those turbulent months. It was not compiled with the intention of serving as a historical document. When the BCRC

122

London office was about to close, Mr Lewinsohn, a thoughtful colleague, gathered together relevant letters, articles and reports. Rather than throw them away, he presented them in a somewhat haphazard order and loosely bound, to Winton, as a reminder and a gesture of thanks for his work and the success of his venture.

As stated in Report 'B' (see the Appendix), the first 'official' group, also accompanied by Chadwick, flew to England on 14 March, the day before the Germans occupied the country. After that, air transports were no longer possible, but trains were still a feasible proposition. To begin with, the children were leaving in relatively small groups and travelled in extra carriages attached to regular passenger trains. As time went on, the numbers rose substantially and special trains had to be provided and paid for. This was no simple task and took a lot of organising. At times, not only the Germans, but even the Czechs made demands and took advantage of the urgency and gravity of the situation, as Winton recalls:

> The Czech railways sometimes threatened to stop the train from leaving unless an extra large sum of money was paid; then I would get an urgent request from Prague for more cash. Although money was extremely tight, somehow we always managed to pay up in time. Some demands the German authorities made were quite ridiculous. 'Have you paid for your dog licence?', was a question sometimes asked. If the reply was 'I have no dog', the unfortunate person was ordered to come back the next day with the proof that he had no dog.

Some of the children I have come across, whose names are missing from the 'official' list, joined one of the transports at the last minute. John Ehrmann and his sister were such a case. The family lived in Prague, but the mother owned and ran a luxury children's home in the Sudetenland. During the Munich crisis she managed to transport all the little beds and bedside cabinets to Prague and to put them in a large flat which happened to be vacant, in the same apartment block where the family lived. This accommodation of about 40 beds she then offered to Doreen Warriner for her destitute children. John remembers how, over the ensuing months, many youngsters came and went. Some were brought to Prague from outlying districts to await the departure of a transport; others were lost or orphaned and had nowhere else to go; the fathers of some of the youngsters had been arrested or murdered, or they were in hiding. A few had managed to get away, leaving their families behind. Some of the children were given false identities and forged documents for their own protection and to facilitate their escape.

The Ehrmanns took a grave risk in harbouring the children, but their help was given freely and willingly. There was, however, one condition: Mrs Ehrmann made Warriner promise that, should the situation worsen, John and his sister would be included in one of the *kindertransports*. Warriner remained true to her word and the children were added at the very last minute to the largest transport of 241 children which arrived in England on 1 July. They came without a sponsor, or a foster family waiting for them, not even a friend. How they managed to get past the British immigration authorities, without such guarantees, no one knows. Possibly with forged documents. John recalls the train's arrival at Liverpool Street Station and the several ladies, probably with Barbara Winton in charge, who sat behind a makeshift table, sorting out such unforseen problems. As John was over 16, they intended to send him to work on a farm, but he had other plans. With dogged determination, he insisted, in his best English, that he and his sister must first complete their education. John so impressed the ladies that he got his way; good homes were found for them both and they were able to carry on with their schooling.

Gerda and Bedrich Loebl were another example. They were due to leave Prague on an early transport, but when it came to the actual departure their mother could not bear to part with them. Is it any wonder? They were only seven and ten years old. However, as the situation grew more and more serious and their father heard rumours that the transports to England were about to cease, he insisted that the children must go. 'We were woken up at midnight and taken straight to the train', Gerda remembers. 'No time really even to say goodbye.' How fortunate that their father stood firm and was not swayed by his distraught wife's pleas. How fortunate that the children were accepted at the twelfth hour.

How fortunate indeed. The next transport – the largest – was due to leave Prague on 1 September 1939. Hitler had invaded Poland that very day and the borders were closed; 250 children were already at the station, but the train was not allowed to depart. The despair of the parents on hearing this fateful decision is unimaginable. As far as it is known, all these children were later deported to concentration camps where they perished, my two young cousins among them.

The declaration of war put an end to the *kindertransports*. For the thousands of endangered children and adults left behind all escape routes were blocked. Winton found some comfort in the knowledge that he had saved as many children as was possible and that whatever happened to them in Britain at least they were safe, but he was devastated that he was powerless to help those who remained in danger.

With the onset of hostilities his duties lay elsewhere. He was always committed to whatever job he took on during his long life; once it was done, it was over – and on to the next thing. It was time to put this episode behind him and to move on. He did just that, most capably, for almost half a century.

THE EMIGRATION GAME – WINTER 1938–39

Mother and I walk through the streets of Prague
Her hands are balled against the falling snow.
(Can't she afford gloves? Are they bare from choice?)
There's snow above and endless steps below.

We have a bag of chocolate-creams; we play
The Emigration Game: England, if brown;
Or, if the centre's white, we must stay here;
If yellow, it's Australia. Snow falls down.

I pick a brown and mother has the white.
She walks with a straight back; Let's try again.
Her legs are varicosed; her heels are raised.
She's bearing up and stout of heart. In vain

From consulate to consulate her steps
Inscribe petitions. Soon the sweets are gone.
Then March comes and invaders bar all routes:
Yet leave no trace of her when they move on;

Their footsteps beating time and bearing down.

Gerda Mayer
From *Bernini's Cat*, a collection of
her poems (Iron Press, 1999).

The Rescue Mission

APPENDIX

MOVEMENT FOR THE CARE OF CHILDREN FROM GERMANY, Ltd.
BRITISH INTER-AID COMMITTEE

Room 61,
BLOOMSBURY HOUSE,
BLOOMSBURY STREET,
LONDON, W.C.1.

Telephone : MUSeum 2900 Ext. 61.

C Z E C H   S E C T I O N

Report 'B' – 2nd October 1939

STATEMENT OF CHILDREN BROUGHT OVER UP TO THE 1ST SEPTEMBER 1939
SHOWING OUR COMMITMENTS FOR RE-EMIGRATION GUARANTEES

Transports from Prague:

1st	14th March 1939	20
2nd	19th April 1939	36
3rd	29th April 1939	29
4th	13th May 1939	61
5th	2nd June 1939	123
6th	1st July 1939	241
7th	20th July 1939	76
8th	2nd August 1939	68
Various transports from Vienna, etc.		15
	Total	669

Specification of obligations:

Before re-emigration deposit required		20
of which – Boys under 12	5	
Girls under 12	13	
Girls over 12	2	

Re-emigration deposits, etc.:

Cheques and cash deposits	83	
Securities	1	
Bank guarantees	50	
Personal guarantees	134	
Other Committees	116	
Movement	28	
Czech Trust Fund	22	
Children's Section	177	591
Children who travelled on own visum		58
	Total	669

The teamwork of concerned volunteers, masterminded by Nicholas Winton, resulted in eight *kindertransports* leaving Prague between 14 March and 2 August 1939, bringing in all 669 endangered children to relative safety in Britain.

This report does not include the 22 children selected by the Barbican Mission, who left for England by air on 12 January when Winton was still in Prague, nor the 29 children whom he helped on their way to Sweden in the care of a beautiful Swedish spy. More surprisingly, the group of children who, according to Doreen Warriner, flew to Britain on 10 March as part of Winton's mission and were accompanied by Chadwick is also not included.

As there are only 591 entries on Winton's long list of names, I assume, rightly or wrongly, that the 78 names which are missing belong to children who travelled on their own visas, or were added to a transport at the last minute. I can certainly confirm that the names and particulars of some of the children who came on the transports have been left out as I have been in contact with approximately 250 Winton children, 12 of whom are not on the list. As this is a considerable percentage, I presume there must be many more.

1. Sir Walter Thomas Layton, an economist and newspaper proprietor, was at that time editor of *The Economist* and chairman of the *News Chronicle*. From 1940–43 he held a key position in the economic direction of the war. He became a peer in 1947.

3 The Re-Awakening

How true, how meaningful were these memorable words spoken by Grete, when she first became aware of her husband's rescue mission. Almost half a century had passed since he had worked at a desperate pace to save young lives, yet all these years he had remained silent and given little, if any, thought to the children he had saved. Had he and Grete not decided to clear the attic, the story may never have been told, and we, the Winton children, would have remained in ignorance of the identity of the man who had played the key role in our rescue.

'You can't throw those papers away ... they are children's lives', said Grete, as she leafed through the now famous scrapbook and the sacred list of names and details of the children brought to Britain back in 1939. Winton agreed, somewhat reluctantly, to try to find a suitable home for the papers. 'I did not think for one moment that they would be of interest to anyone so long after it happened', he explained.

At first, no one seemed to want the documentation, but that situation changed dramatically when he turned to Dr Elizabeth Maxwell, the French wife of the late newspaper tycoon, Robert Maxwell, a Czech-Jew by birth. As Winton drove towards Headington Hill Hall, the Maxwells' gracious Oxford home, he could not have guessed how significant this day would be and what far-reaching changes to his life it would bring.

Dr Maxwell was intrigued by his story, fascinated by the documents and impressed with Winton as a man – his modesty, sincerity, warmth of heart and his sharp dry wit. It is to her credit that, in February 1988, the news of his deed reached millions of homes. The story, under the title 'Lost Children' was featured across several pages of the *Sunday Mirror*, one of her husband's tabloids, and was highlighted on the same day by Esther Rantzen, the television producer, on her popular programme *That's Life*.

Winton was invited to the studio totally unaware of the reason for his attendance. Esther had asked me to take part in the programme and had given me a brief outline of the course it would take; I received strict instructions not to let Winton know who I was and not to move from my seat, as my story was an essential part of the programme. Winton certainly did not envisage that the history of his rescue mission was about to unfold before his eyes and invade millions of homes. He had no idea that next to him and behind him were a few of the 'lost children', and was more than a little annoyed that I ignored his request to change places with Rudy Wesselly, the one person he recognised in the audience. Rudy Wesselly and Winton were co-members of the National Committee of the Abbeyfield Society. From an article in the society's bulletin Rudy had learnt about Winton's pre-war role and thus discovered the identity of his rescuer – the first 'child' to do so.

Now, overwhelmed by Winton's presence, my thoughts and emotions in a whirl, unable to believe that this was real, I sat next to him, stonefaced, ignoring his request. I had searched for this man for so long.

The story was presented sensitively and poignantly. Winton was greatly moved, yet the unexpectedness, the shock of seeing the events unfold on the screen and then finding himself sitting next to three of *his* children could have had dire consequences. He was, after all, not in the prime of his life; he was in his eightieth year. The element of surprise played heavily on his emotions and touched the hearts of not only those in the audience, but an enormous number of viewers, many of whom recall the programme to this day. For me, it was an incredible moment as we embraced and I was able, at long last, to thank him for my life. Neither of us guessed then how our lives would change and how closely they would be linked in the years ahead.

That night Winton's happiness at finding himself in the midst of a small group of some of those he had saved was marred by learning the cruel truth that, as far as it is known, none of the 250 children who were prevented from leaving Prague the day Hitler invaded Poland had survived. Until then, he was unaware of the tragedy.

GETTING ACQUAINTED

The initial publicity, followed by further articles and television appearances resulted in a flood of letters and phone-calls from many Winton children anxious to meet their rescuer. The numbers rose rapidly and were augmented to over 150 by several dozen of my former school friends whose names I identified on Winton's list.

Dr Maxwell had organised an international scholars' conference 'Remembering for the Future' to be held in Oxford the following July. The major theme of the conference was the impact of the Holocaust on contemporary civilisations and Jewish/Christian relations. A meeting of survivors, at which both Robert and Elizabeth Maxwell were present, at the start of the conference provided a splendid opportunity for as many Winton children as possible to get together. They came from as far as the United States and Israel, and my sister journeyed from New Zealand.

On Dr Maxwell's suggestion, we presented Winton with 'our' scrapbook – a medley of letters and testimonies from his new ever-grateful and ever-growing family. With contributions from the participants, Dr Maxwell kindly purchased a gold ring on our behalf inscribed with words 'Save One Life – Save the World'. The money raised exceeded the cost of the ring and Winton, typically, remembered the old folk at Winton House, the Abbeyfield home in Windsor named after him and chose to present them with a piano, which is there to this day.

WHAT BECAME OF THE CHILDREN?

Winton may have dismissed us children from his mind during all those years, but so many of us had often wondered who had masterminded our rescue and how it came about. We were, therefore, thrilled and greatly moved to discover his identity at last, to hear him speak and to have the opportunity to lift the veil from the mystery of the rescue mission and, what is more, to be able to thank him for our lives. 'I didn't want thanks', Winton said. 'It is enough to know that you are alive, that you are happy and well, that you are making the best of your lives. My one regret is that I could not have saved more.'

He was warmed by the response of the majority, by their positive outlook, particularly by such remarks as 'Thank you for my wife', or 'Thank you for the last 50 years'. Winton now recalls:

> When I met the children again, I learnt that for a long time some could not forgive their parents because they did not understand how they could send them away. They felt abandoned, the young ones especially. Happily, such comments were rare. Then there were the few who criticised their adoptive parents. To them, I replied 'I gave you the chance of life'.

We all grasped that chance because we felt that the best way to repay our parents for making the ultimate sacrifice, by letting us, their children, go, was to make the most of our lives. The happiness and fulfilment we could achieve would ensure that their sacrifice and Nicky's valiant efforts would not have been in vain. The loss of our parents is part of who and what we are; the past still returns to haunt us. As one Winton child replied to schoolchildren who asked if she had cried on hearing that her parents had perished: 'Yes, I cried, I am still crying today.'

'Mr Winton' became Nicky, a father-figure, a dear friend to all of us who met him; he gave us back a vital part of our history. From then on, I became increasingly involved in his life and all matters concerning the children and the rescue mission.

Nicky is a modest man; he did not seek, nor want publicity and has been embarrassed by all the acclaim and hero-worship he received during those heady months in 1988, which turned his normally peaceful life into a whirl of activity. In his mind he still minimised the importance of his deed. A letter from Karel Reisz, the film and theatre producer and director, made him realise the importance of his appearance in our lives:

I was in the United States at the time of your first broadcast and only returned to catch the second. I was very moved by the story of your participation in the children's trains from Czechoslovakia – because I think I was on the first train.

I was 12 years old at that time and had always thought that the whole organisation had been in the hands of the Quakers. I had no knowledge of your special responsibility and now write to thank you from the depth of my heart for your great work to which I directly owe my life.

Yesterday evening was especially moving for me because Sunday night is the night my three sons come to dinner at our house with their wives and children. Your appearance on the TV programme provoked all manner of reminiscences. Many of the things that happened at that time were suddenly brought back and I was able – it is 49 years after the event, after all – to recall for them something of my own heritage – and therefore theirs. We all came to realise very vividly and somehow concretely through your appearance on the TV screen that not only I, but my children, Matthew, Toby and Barney, all owe our very existence to your wonderful efforts in 1939! They join me in sending you our most humble thanks. My debt to you is very great indeed.

My sense of gratitude to this country, and especially to the fine, decent things and people which even now underpin so much of my life here, has deepened over the years. This is one of the things my children, who are inclined to be critical in the way of the rebellious young, have never quite understood. Last night, your appearance

133

on TV brought home to them, once again and most vividly, that this is a generous country, generous and humane; we spoke into the early hours of the morning of all those tragic days, of the dreadful events which formed me.

I hope that you are able to derive the pleasure you so amply deserve from contemplating the happiness you have created for so many of us.

This was the first of many moving letters and personal visits from *his* grateful children. Gradually he began to learn about their lives after their arrival in Britain. To date, more than 250 of the 669 former child refugees have been in touch.

NEW BEGINNINGS

Every Winton child has a story to tell. Our experiences, good and bad, were varied and our way of coping as diverse as the behaviour and attitudes of the people who took us in. Let us take a glimpse into some of their lives and situations since their dramatic departure from Prague.

How many of us today would be prepared to take in a child, a foreigner whose background and family were unknown to us and whom we had never met and take on the responsibility for that child for an unlimited period without outside financial or social help?

It is amazing that so many came forward, from all walks of life, rich and poor, Christian and Jewish. The British – particularly at that time – were incredibly charitable and compassionate, yet their unselfish brave decision to help could not have been easy. I think my foster-father's reasons for offering his home and heart to me speak for many others:

I knew I could not save the world, or stop the war from coming, but I knew I could save one human soul. As Chamberlain broke his pledge to Czechoslovakia and Jews were in the greatest danger, I decided it must be a Czech, Jewish child.

When it comes to a generous heart and self-sacrifice, I do not think there is anyone to match the late Miss Harder. In 1939, she was a 54-year-old spinster running a little shop next to Archway Station in north London. She lived in a tiny flat with very limited means. Desperate to help, she continually turned up at Winton's office, offering to foster a child. Although the Committee were touched by her desire to help, they were loathe to place a youngster in her care – on account of her age, single status and meagre income.

On Winton's list were the three Gumpel sisters, whose mother had requested that they stay together. Winton and his helpers had given up hope of finding a family willing to take all three and, in desperation, offered them to Miss Harder. To everyone's amazement, she jumped at the chance, even refusing the Committee's offer of financial help, in case this would deprive another child of a safe home.

Fifteen-year-old Laura (then Hannelore) and her two younger sisters arrived at Liverpool Street Station where they were warmly embraced by Barbara Winton, then handed over to a shabbily dressed lady who took them to her dark, dismal two-roomed flat which she shared with a couple of dogs. It was typical of Miss Harder's nature to give the girls her bedroom whilst she slept on the sofa in the living room.

In the first few weeks it was very difficult for the girls to adjust and they were thoroughly miserable and very homesick, although their foster-mother did all she could to make them happy.

When the sisters received a message that their mother had been imprisoned as a hostage for their father, who had fled to Poland, Miss Harder's love and compassion and efforts to console them brought them close. Tragically, six months after the arrival of the girls this devoted foster-mother died of consumption. The sisters were separated; Laura went into domestic service until 1942 when she joined the Auxiliary Territorial Service (ATS). Foster families were found for the two younger girls. Their mother perished in the camps.

After the war the younger girls emigrated to the United States where they had successful careers in the field of education. Laura worked as a secretary and in 1949 married Walter Selo, a fellow refugee. She tells her story in her moving autobiography *Three Lives in Transit* (Excalibur, 1992). Now widowed, she lives alone in her north London flat, which she rarely leaves due to health problems.

* * *

When in September 1939, Winton had to give up the running of the Czech Children Section, his mother, who was already very much involved in the aftercare of the children, took over her son's duties. An immensely capable woman, with a down-to-earth, no-nonsense attitude, she came into her own, and excelled at sorting out individual problems and difficulties for both foster parents and their charges. Those whom she helped have nothing but the highest praise for her.

Of course, everything did not always go smoothly. The following most extraordinary and quite inexplicable incident occurred when the last comparatively small transport of 68 children reached Liverpool Street Station on 2 August 1939.

Ten-year-old Hugo Meisl (now Marom) and his brother Rudy aged nine, together with their friends, the three Tomaschoff boys, had left for England convinced that their parents would soon follow. In their case, it was Hugo's father, not Winton, who found a home and a guarantor for them all. Hugo recalls:

> For reasons which we could not understand then, out of all the children we, the five boys from Brno, were not met by anyone. We sat on the platform on our suitcases, from morning till night until a taxi driver, who had driven past the platform a number of times and had seen us waiting, came over and asked what had happened. As I knew a little English, I explained that a certain Mr Rabinovitz was supposed to have sent someone to pick us up and that we did not know his address or that of the hostel in which we were to stay. As we were starving, he took the five of us in his cab to a fish and chip shop for the first hot meal since our departure. We spent the next two nights in his two-roomed flat with his wife and baby.

Next morning, the taxi driver drove us around the East End looking for the Jewish hostel, orphanage or boarding school which was expecting us. Not until the third day did he find a German refugee children's hostel in Cricklewood which was willing to accept us, although we were Czechs. We stayed at this hostel for a few weeks only, in a very unfriendly environment, until we were evacuated to Bedford with all the other English schoolchildren from the Harben Elementary School in Swiss Cottage.

As each transport was usually met by Winton, together with his mother and other helpers, he is at a loss to understand how such a thing could have happened. He was unaware of this incident at the time.

After the war, Hugo made considerable, but unsuccessful efforts to find the kind taxi driver; but he did find another man to whom the five boys are indebted – their guarantor, a Mr Otto Kubie, who, with his wife and three children, were also refugees. He had deposited £50 for each of the five boys and did not have sufficient money left to travel from Glasgow to London to meet them; he presumed that Rabbi Rabinowitz would be waiting for them. This, the rabbi failed to do, nor did he ever bother to contact the boys.

COPING WITH LONELINESS

Some children who were placed in hostels, training farms and other such institutions faced more problems in adjusting than those who went to families. They had the advantage of sharing their lives with others in the same situation, but the impersonal, totally alien environment was difficult to handle.

By the time Harry Warschauer boarded one of Winton's trains he was an experienced refugee, having already fled with his parents from Nazi persecution, first from Berlin to the Sudetenland, then to the Czech capital. At the age of 15 he started his new life in England on a Youth Aliyah Training Farm, where he was taught farming, gardening and finally carpentry.

His inability to settle triggered by homesickness, augmented by loneliness, brought him to the edge of despair.

His unhappiness was so profound that a little more than a year after his arrival, he took an overdose. Fortunately, he was found in time and, without any further ado, was taken to Barbara Winton who gave him a brisk, no-nonsense lecture on survival and optimism. 'She was wonderful', Harry recalls with heart-felt gratitude. 'She told me to get on with my life and be positive. It must have worked, because I never attempted suicide again.'

Work it did indeed. Far from remaining a farmer or carpenter, Harry progressed to Fleet Street, numerous journalistic accolades and a happy marriage.

When, in 1988, Harry realised for the first time that it was Barbara Winton's son who had organised his escape, the powerful, long-buried memories brought such emotional trauma that he did not contact Winton until a year later on his own sixty-fifth birthday. 'I simply thought – I am 65 – I have made it. I have enjoyed these last 50 years and I owe them all to him. I am so glad that at last I have been able to tell him that.' Sadly, Harry did not live to see the publication of this book. He died on 12 July 2001, aged 76.

* * *

I learnt how lonely a foreigner can feel in a totally English environment through the experiences of my sister, Eva (Hayman, née Diamant). At the beginning of 1940 I was invited to spend a week at the exclusive Church of England boarding school whose headmistress was her sponsor. The beautiful grounds and buildings, the facilities for study and sport, the elegant uniforms, the opulence of the whole place were in sharp contrast to the cold grey church hall which temporarily housed four classes for my fellow Liverpool evacuees. How I envied her! Yet I guessed even then that being in a 'posh' school did not necessarily bring understanding and happiness. I also became aware of how lucky I was to have an older sister in England who encouraged me and worried about me throughout the war years

– the one person there who knew and missed our parents, as I did. She was my guardian angel, my rock – my one link with home, as I describe in my diary:

> The days with Eva flew by. On Saturday, I had to leave. I thought my heart would break. On the way to the station I couldn't stop crying. Eva tried to console me though she too was near to tears. Darling Eva! How she encourages me and guides me when often she herself is in need of encouragement and advice. There isn't a better dearer sister in the whole wide world!

However, I did not know how deeply troubled she was and would remain. Eva recalls:

> As we left at the end of June 1939, the predominant feeling was unhappiness that we had to go, leaving our parents behind (I was 15 and my sister Vera almost 11). I know we will come back – but will we? I know I have to be brave, but how can I be? I was so apprehensive at the uncertainty.
>
> At school I felt different, particularly to begin with. I was always 'the refugee'. Everyone was very kind and I felt accepted by them, especially the family who took me in during the holidays, but I was never one of them: everywhere I went I was 'their friend from Czechoslovakia'. But worrying about my parents once war started overshadowed everything else. I didn't want people's pity, so I didn't tell anyone how I felt and was, therefore, very lonely and isolated in my anxiety.

In those early years of the war, I did not dream how much more fortunate I was to be than Eva. After the fall of France in May 1940 the Czechoslovak Government in Exile and members of the forces as well as civilian families who had sought refuge in France fled again, this time to Britain. Soon afterwards a Czechoslovak school was founded, which changed the lives of more than 200 child refugees in Britain, including myself. In the autumn of 1941, as I climbed the sweeping stairway of Hinton

Hall, an old Shropshire manor, my isolation from all things Czech was, at last, coming to an end.

This book is not the place to describe in detail the life and meaning of the school. I have covered the subject at length in my autobiography, *Pearls of Childhood*. It was more than a school; it was our home. We were bound together, both children and staff, because we were all refugees waiting for the war to end. Those of us who had come on the *kindertransports* shared our hopes and fears and thus eased the pain of waiting. We were, in truth, like an extended family and the ties forged during those wartime years have survived to this day. We were taught both in English and Czech and the staff ensured that our Czech identity was not lost and that the spark of patriotism never went out.

Our numbers grew and eventually half of the pupils in the primary school moved to Maesfen Hall near Nantwich, whilst the gymnasium (grammar school) took over the Abernant Hotel, in Llanwrtyd Wells in Wales.

Eva came to visit whilst I was still at Hinton Hall; by then she had left her school and had started nursing. She wrote to me, describing her feelings:

> I felt I belonged. I was with you and I truly loved you. I was with people who had the same problems. We were all refugees in a strange land, hoping the day would come when we could return home.
>
> At my school and then in the hospital I was the foreigner – they couldn't understand my feelings even if I tried to explain. At Hinton Hall, people just knew. I did not envy you your life, but I did so want to share in it, and to study. I did not at that time like nursing and was not happy in my work. I was almost happy at your school – as much as any of us could be.

Soon after Eva's return to the hospital in Poole, she was put on the wards for the war wounded and was proud to be helping the war effort. She continued with her nursing career throughout her working life.

When war ended Eva was the first to hear that our mother

had survived, but, ironically, had later died of typhus after the liberation of Bergen-Belsen and that our father had been shot on a death march. Her world and future – and mine – fell apart. Eva told me that the hardest part of hearing about mother, apart from the shock, was how to soften the blow for me, help me to reconcile myself to our loss.

Eva returned to Prague for a few months in 1945/46. She recalls:

> My stay there feels very unreal now. I never cried. It didn't really hit me, I couldn't face it, but I coped fairly well in 1945. I was younger and stronger and still full of THEM, determined to do what they would have wanted of me. But I was living in a daze.
>
> When I returned the second time in 1975, I found myself reliving 1939 and I couldn't cope, because my life was being torn in all directions. I was so unhappy, because only then I really said goodbye to my parents.
>
> I had to accept what happened. I feel my parents would hate me to harbour feelings of not forgiving and of resentment, as such feelings would only damage me. I have tried not to feel bitter, but that does not mean I have succeeded.

Eva, now divorced, was married to an English doctor and emigrated to New Zealand in 1956. For years she suffered with depression and indecisiveness which did not improve until she took a degree course in counselling, faced her past and counselled herself. Writing her autobiography *By the Moon and the Stars* (Random House, New Zealand, 1989) completed, as far as it is possible, her rehabilitation.

* * *

The experiences and attitude of another Winton child, Eva Gasper (née Werner), were in some ways similar to, in other ways quite different from, those of my sister. In a letter to her rescuer Eva wrote:

I had been 'adopted' by a school in Stourbridge, Worcestershire, but the staff wisely decided that I should live with one of the pupils and I was placed with a widow and her only daughter of my own age. I had left my own family and stepped straight into the warmth of another. We were both only children, we took one look at each other and knew that we had found the joy of having a sister. Sadly, cancer has claimed both the mother and daughter, but it was a relationship I shall cherish to the end of my days. After School Certificate I worked on a farm and while tending some sick calves it dawned on me that I could do this for humans and, thus, I found my niche in life – nursing.

In 1947 I, a Czech, met an Armenian and after qualifying followed him to India. His parents had also been refugees and had fled there from Turkey where the Armenians were being massacred early on in the century. They had no Mr Winton to organise a transport for them, but travelled in biblical fashion on a donkey, with the first of their eight children. We lived four and a half years in Calcutta where both my children were born. We came to live in England permanently in 1953. My husband and I had many plans for retirement, but sadly he contracted Parkinson's disease and was ill for many years – he died three years ago.

The marvel for me has been to have had the chance to live – it has truly been a fantastic experience.

NO HUGS, NO KISSES

Some children found it exceedingly hard to adapt to their new life in England, to the families who were complete strangers, to the foreign language, food and customs, and the natural reserve of the British. They were consumed by homesickness, yearning for their parents and friends, hating the isolation and separation from everything that was familiar. A show of physical affection was often absent and sorely missed; to many, hugs and kisses

142

would have made the world of difference, particularly to the little ones.

In most cases, relationships with foster families were warm and affectionate, but without emotion. We were used to loving homes, where there was no emotional restraint. It was impossible for us to understand that our foster-parents were doing their best not to replace our real parents and in any way alienate us from our former environment. My foster-mother was affectionate and caring, but careful not to take over my mother's role, her one wish and aim being to hand me back one day. In 1939 no one dreamt that the war would last six years and that many of us would not return to our homeland. There was, therefore, no feeling of permanence; it was well into the war before it dawned on us that our separation could be be forever.

As we have already seen, some children handled their situation well – others had great difficulty. Lenka, who was nine years old on arrival, said:

> The only way I could cope was by blotting out the past. I tried so hard that ultimately I succeeded and soon became the little daughter my foster-parents had always wanted. In a matter of two years I even forgot my Czech and when, a year later, I went to the Czech school, I was miserable and insecure and begged my English mother to take me back home.

When the end of the war was in sight, Lenka was apprehensive about the possibility of being uprooted again and forced to leave the family she had grown to love and regard as her own and restart life in what would now be, to her, an alien country, whose language she could no longer understand. However, Lenka's parents perished in the Holocaust.

> Of course, I didn't want to lose them, I hoped they would survive, but I barely remembered them and, in a way, I was relieved, yet ashamed, that I wouldn't have to make a decision and face such a problem, and that I could carry on with my happy life in Britain.

Lenka's friends always assumed she was the natural daughter of her foster-parents; she continued living under this false identity blocking out her past until 1988 when Winton came into our lives. Only then did she find the strength to turn to her roots, throw away the cloak of pretence and admit to the world, but more importantly to herself, who she really was, and to weep and grieve at long last over an irretrievable loss.

* * *

The following story illustrates how even the second generation can be affected. Fourteen-year-old William, who came from the Sudetenland, just made it to England on the last transport. Boys of his age were hard to place and no one had come forward with an offer of a home. In desperation, his Czech aunt, who spoke English, found people with the same name from a London telephone book and contacted them pleading for a home for her nephew. Her ingenuity paid off. William was taken in by a Jewish family, who were kind and provided him with an excellent education, but showed him little affection. Lonely and isolated, he left his boarding school as soon as he was old enough and joined the Royal Air Force. A chance meeting with a friendly soldier from Yorkshire led to an invitation to his parents' home. The welcome William received there whenever on leave made him feel one of the family. At long last he had an anchor. At the same house he met, fell in love with, and later married a Yorkshire girl whose parents treated him like a son. By the time war ended, he looked upon Yorkshire as home and the love and friendliness he found there eased the pain of losing his own parents. But the pain of the past is something he cannot face to this day.

William's daughter, Carol, is trying to find out and record as much as she can in order that the family is not forgotten. She explains:

> Father is more English than the English. He so wanted to belong, not to be different. He even talks with a Yorkshire accent. I can understand his feelings. Before he left Prague,

144

his parents were not wanted by the Czechs because they were ethnic Germans, though they were Czech citizens, nor by the Germans because they were Jews.

How can I feel totally English with such a background? I have always known that there was some Jewish blood in the family and that we mustn't talk about it to anyone. I know that my grandparents perished, as had the majority of Dad's family ... I had a normal childhood – warm, secure, a loving home, but then there were so few other relatives ... I can't remember ever not knowing, but Father just doesn't want to remember. I find talking about the past, even to you, like breaking a trust. I feel guilty. Father copes with the past extremely well, or so it seems, by blotting it out, but I feel if he opened the floodgates, God knows what would happen. I think I am having to grieve for my father because he can't do it for himself.

A newspaper article in spring 1998 about our rescuer prompted William to agree to meet Winton at my home. The conversation flowed, but that early painful part of William's life was avoided.

* * *

Kindness was experienced by many of the children. My friend Uta Klein (née Reicherova) was eight years old when she went to live with her foster family in Manchester. They had three grown-up children and only two bedrooms, plus a boxroom. Uta had to share with 26-year-old Irene not only the tiny boxroom, but also her bed, to which Irene consented willingly. Who would act so unselfishly, so big-heartedly today?

Uta, who came from an affluent, middle-class home recalls, still with a little shudder, the unpleasant feel of the hard flannelette sheets and the coarse felt blankets which, to her sensitive skin, felt like barbed wire, her shock at the tiny semi and at the drabness of her new home. But she soon learned to love and appreciate this kind family prepared to squeeze into their home an unknown little girl. When war ended and the news came that Uta's parents had not survived, they wanted to adopt her.

The security and happiness found within her adoptive family and at the Czech school, which she joined, coupled with the presence in England of a young, caring uncle, had a very positive influence on Uta's life. She retained contact with the family but now, sadly, only Irene remains. Uta is a widow – she married a fellow refugee from Germany with whom she had two sons. Her bubbly personality, optimistic outlook and *joie de vivre* has never left her and endears her to everyone she meets; none more than Winton whose face lights up with pleasure at the very mention of her name.

FORGING A BOND WITH THOSE IN NEED

'I always had a lot of feeling for the underdog – for someone who was different', Nicky once told me. As a youngster, Nicky, himself an outsider, identified and sympathised with those who did not quite conform. Similarly many of 'his children' forged a bond with those in need and chose caring professions – social workers, doctors, nurses, educationalists and preachers. In retirement many have taken up voluntary work (as has Nicky). Could this be a consequence of learning to live as outsiders from such an early age? Of being completely dependent on the generosity and kindness of the British? Of knowing the pain of being the victims?

* * *

Vera Schaufeld (née Loewy) was nine years old when Germany occupied Czechoslovakia. Her mother, a doctor, was German, her father, an adviser to the Czechoslovak government on international law. He was also head of the Jewish community (which was not orthodox) in his native town of Klatovy, near Pilzen.

Vera remembers vividly her father's temporary arrest the day the Germans marched in, her fear and her first taste of anti-

146

Semitism. 'When I told my teacher I was going to England, she replied, "Jews are always the first to run away".'

In Britain, Vera went to live with an affluent Church of England family. She attended church and went to a Methodist boarding school. The kindness of her guardian, who also tried to make her feel good about being Jewish, compensated a little for the attitude of his wife who constantly expected Vera to show gratitude.

> I loathed accepting everything as presents, having to be grateful all the time. Being in this situation seemed so demeaning, such a contrast to my own home. Any fondness I felt for her evaporated when, after a British soldier was killed in Palestine, she remarked, with tactless cruelty, 'perhaps Hitler knew what he was doing when he killed all the Jews'.

When war ended, Vera was filled with mixed emotions:

> I was worried because I had forgotten my Czech and German, worried whether I would be able to take my School Certificate the following year, but then I thought, none of this matters. All I want is to see my parents. I never thought they would be dead; it was a complete, devastating shock.

After training to be a teacher, Vera decided to go to Israel. 'I was still very uncertain about my Jewish identity and wanted to find out what it is to be Jewish, what it means, if you don't believe in God, and I don't. But one feels Jewish.'

In Israel, Vera met and married Avron, a survivor of Auschwitz and Buchenwald. After losing her first baby, they went to England for a holiday and decided to make their home there.

Vera, who specialised in English as a Second Language, eventually became responsible for teachers of ESL and for placing them in schools. She held this post until her retirement. 'I felt a very strong affinity for children who had to leave their homes, learn a new language and a new culture.'

147

Vera returned to Czechoslovakia only once – in 1976:

> I felt nothing for the people in Klatovy. Father was so well
> known there, he had lived there all his life, yet they didn't
> save a single book of his – nothing was left. I went into
> what had been our home, into my nursery. The old stove,
> the washbasin, the rings for my swing were still there. I
> found my way to my old school and to the synagogue
> which, of course, is now closed. How could I feel anything?
> Father was born there, he'd spent his whole life there, but
> no one cared. How could I feel anything – not a word of
> Czech came back to me.

Vera and Avron frequent the London Survivor's Centre
where they find comfort in being amongst people who had
similar experiences. Giving talks to schoolchildren on her life
and the *kindertransports* helps her to cope and gives her
tremendous satisfaction.

* * *

When 11-year-old Sue Pearson (née Ehrmann) was told she
could go to England, she was adamant that she would not leave
without her parents.

> Somehow I was persuaded and, I suppose, the knowledge
> that I would be coming with 14 Red Falcons helped. The
> British Woodcraft Folk, who have ties with the Red Falcons,
> had been able to find families to allow 20 children to come
> from Prague. I seem to have totally obliterated the parting
> from my parents, even to the extent of not understanding
> for many years why railway stations made me so sad.
>   This separation from anybody else I knew, anyone at all
> who had been involved in my previous life, has had a
> profound effect on me. No one to remember with, to
> reminisce with, is like losing one's history. I had a very
> patchy education and had to leave school at the age of 14,
> which I resented.

Maidstone Central European Refugee Fund.

Chairman:
Rev. A. O. STANDEN, M.A.
The Vicarage, Maidstone.

Hon. Treasurer:
A. B. HOMAN, Esq.,
Westminster Bank,
Maidstone.

Hon. Secretary:
Rev. C. E. REED,
124 Loose Road,
Maidstone.

RUGBY (CHRISTADELPHIAN) REFUGEE COMMITTEE

Associated with the Movement for the Care of Children from Germany,
Bloomsbury House, Bloomsbury Street, London, W.C.1.

Telephone: RUGBY 2614 (day)
RUGBY 9383 (night)

Hon. Treasurer:
GEO. PASS,
Hamilton Rise,
Packington Road,
Ashby-de-la-Zouch.

Hon. Secretary:
R. A. OVERTON,
The Green,
Bilton,
Rugby.

Please Quote...............

WORTHING REFUGEE COMMITTEE

President: HIS WORSHIP THE MAYOR

Cheltenham Committee for Aiding Refugee Children

AFFILIATED TO THE MOVEMENT FOR CARE OF REFUGEE CHILDREN FROM GERMANY
LONDON.

WIRRAL REFUGEE COMMITTEE

Chairman:
REV. B. P. ROBIN.

Treasurer:
DR. C. O. STALLYBRASS.

Secretary:
MISS E. M. CRAM.

Stoke-on-Trent Central Committee for Refugees.

PATRONS:
BISHOP OF STAFFORD
ARCHDEACON OF STOKE-ON-TRENT
COL. J. C. WEDGWOOD, M.P.
ALD. ARTHUR HOLLINS, M.P.
LONDON REPRESENTATIVE:
MRS. L. KAHN-FREUND.

CHAIRMAN:
DR. B. STROSS
Telephone 3088

JOINT TREASURERS:
MR. C. WILTSHAW
DR. B. STROSS

HON. SECRETARY:
MR. C. WILTSHAW
CARLTON WORKS
STOKE-ON-TRENT
Telephone 4205

MANCHESTER CHILD REFUGEE COMMITTEE

MOVEMENT FOR THE CARE OF CHILDREN FROM GERMANY.

EALING 3030.
Telephone

REFUGEE COMMITTEE

TOWN HALL,
EALING, W.5.

17. Examples of other committees in operation at the time.

BRITISH COMMITTEE for REFUGEES from CZECHOSLOVAKIA
CHILDREN'S SECTION

Telephone: MUSeum 2900 Ext. 217

BLOOMSBURY HOUSE,
Room 217,
BLOOMSBURY STREET,
LONDON, W.C.1.

18. Contents page of document containing particulars of 400 urgent cases, produced by the British Committee for Refugees from Czechoslovakia, Children's Section.

Particulars of 400 urgent cases.

Nationality.

Sudeten Germany	91
Germany	82
Austria	121
Slovakia	38
Czechoslovakia	68
	400

The country of origin has been taken where the children are stateless.

Jewish	364
not Jewish	34
father arrested	21
father or mother dead	46
both parents dead or in orphanage	18
father or mother unfit through illness	32
emigration possibilities for parents	41
expelled	124
live apart from their parents	36
father fled, address unknown	7
father or mother already in England or abroad	16
morally endangered	9

This document of identity is issued with the approval of His Majesty's Government in the United Kingdom to young persons to be admitted to the United Kingdom for educational purposes under the care of the Inter-Aid Committee for children.

THIS DOCUMENT REQUIRES NQ VISA.

PERSONAL PARTICULARS.

Name BERMANN   THOMAS

Sex MALE   Date of Birth 15.2.34.

Place KÖNIGGRÄTZ

Full Names and Address of Parents

BERMANN   KARL & LENKA

U. NACHODA

HRONOV M/MET

BRITISH COMMITTEE FOR CHILDREN
IN PRAGUE.

---

19. Young person's document of identity, issued by the United Kingdom (both sides shown).

This side is reserved for official use only:—

LEAVE TO LAND GRANTED AT HARWICH
THIS DAY ON CONDITION THAT THE HOLDER
DOES NOT ENTER ANY EMPLOYMENT
PAID OR UNPAID WHILE IN THE UNITED
KINGDOM

6014

Durchreisesichtvermerk
für Bermann Thomas
(Name des Inhabers)
zur Reise durch das Reichsgebiet — und zurück —
über die Grenzübergangsstelle(n)

Der Sichtvermerk kann zum Grenzübertritt bis zum
10. Juni 1939 einschließlich benutzt werden.
Reisefrist: Tage | Die Durchreise muß innerhalb von 03 Tagen von
vom Grenzübertritt ab | Grenzübertritt ab erfolgen

Prag, den 27. Mai 1939

der DEUTSCHEN GESANDTSCHAFT
in PRAG.

BRITISH COMMITTEE FOR CHILDREN IN PRAGUE

Hon.Sec. T.R. Creighton

Prague XII, Rubesova 17

P.T.

Please complete the following:

1. The transport no. of ....is:
2. We enclose 3 labels, each with your child's number.
3. The luggage must be sent on ....at.........
   from ....Station in Prague.
4. Each child is allowed only 2 suitcases and each must have a luggage label.
5. The luggage must only contain clothes. Should the Customs have objections to a case, the child to whom it belongs will be excluded and taken off the Register.
6. The child may take only a rucksack for the journey - with food and drink, washing things and perhaps a small blanket.
7. The third label must be tied safely round the child's neck, before he or she arrives at the station.
8. Each child can bring only 10 marks in coins.
9. The ticket to London costs K590.- for children under 10 years old K295.- The Gewman transit visa costs K24.- for each child. Please send this amount as soon as possible by postal order to our office in Prague. So, for children over 10, K614.-, and children under 10, K319.- In cases when the parents indicate they can't afford to pay, they must prove bad poverty.
10. At departure, the children must sit in the seat with their number. Nobody must enter the train - except those bringing children under 8. As soon as the transport list has been checked with the children in each carriage, the children may get out on to the platform. It is therefore imperative that the children stay in their places during the checking of the list.
11. The train leaves from ....Station ON .... AT .... All children must be at the station .... before that time. The children whose pass and/or luggage label have not been given to us, must do so immediately.
12. At the moment it is not necessary for a child to have a passport, but if the child already has one, it should be brought and given to the representative at the station.
13. All necessary documents for the journey will be taken care of by us.
14. Under no circumstances can pleas to pay the journey for poor children be accepted.
15. Please follow all the above instructions exactly.

20. Instructions for parents of children leaving on the *kindertransports*.

MOVEMENT FOR THE CARE OF CHILDREN FROM GERMANY LTD.

CZECH SECTION.

Bloomsbury House,

Room 61,

Bloomsbury Street

Telephone Museum 2900, Ext.61.   London, W.C.1.

Dear Sir/Madam,

As the child previously guaranteed by you cannot come over to this country owing to the war, we are wondering whether you would extend your offer of hospitality to any other refugee child from Czechoslovakia already in England.

A large number of children was already brought over to England by our transports. For various reasons, owing to war conditions, we have to find new hospitality for some of these children whenever their present foster parents cannot keep them any longer.

Would you be prepared to help? If so, kindly fill in the attached questionaire regarding particulars re sex, age, religion, etc. of the child to whom you wish to give hospitality. Please return this form when completed to:

Mrs. B. Winton,
"The Grange"
Hindhead, Surrey.

Your name will then be added to the index of hospitality offers, and Mrs. Winton who is in charge for the after-care of children from Czechoslovakia in this country will approach you whenever a child fitting with your offer might have to be re-placed.

Thanking you for your kind attention and assistance that you may give us in our work,

Yours faithfully,

W. M. LOEWINSOHN.

Asst. Sec.
CZECH CHILDREN'S SECTION.

21. Letter from the Movement for the Care of Children from Germany Ltd, Czech Section, showing Winton's mother's involvement.

22. Winton with one of his 'children', the late Harry Warschauer, 1989.

23. The 1990 school reunion in Wales – Joe Schlesinger, one of the children, with Winton.

24. Winton with some of the children he saved. From left to right: Olga (USA), Alice (Czech Republic), Nicholas Winton, Eva (Berlin), Rennee (USA) and Vera Gissing.

25. The Wintons in Prague in 1991, when Nicholas was awarded the Honorary Citizenship of Prague.

26. In Prague in 1991, a guest of the Jewish community.

27. Winton having been presented with the Honorary Freedom of the Royal Borough of Windsor and Maidenhead, April 1999.

28. October 1999, group in Prague to celebrate Barbara Winton's birthday. Back row, left to right: Tom Schrecker (Winton child), Vera Gissing, Winton's daughter Barbara, Nicholas Winton, Doris Koziskova. Front row, left to right: Matej Minac, his wife Karen and Martina Stolbova, Matej's assistant.

29. Press conference prior to the premiere of *All My Loved Ones*, October 1999, Prague. Front row from left to right: Dagmar Simova, Nicholas Winton, Vera Gissing, Alice Klimova, Helena Faltisova (Winton children living in Prague). Back row left to right: Uta Klein (Britain), Tom Schrecker (Australia), both Winton children, Matej Minac, Joe Schlesinger, Jiri Vejvoda.

30. Nicholas Winton, Joe Schlesinger and Vera Gissing with Vaclav Klaus, the former Head of Parliament, after the premiere of *All My Loved Ones*, Prague, October 1999.

31. Nicky and Grete celebrate their fiftieth wedding anniversary with their grandchildren, Laurence and Holly, October 1998.

32. Nicholas Winton, Eva Hayman (Vera Gissing's sister) and Vera outside Vera Gissing's cottage during the filming of *Into the Arms of Strangers*, in which Winton and Vera's sister both feature. Nicholas' role in the film was relatively small, but he was the only rescuer to feature in it.

33. The premiere of *Into the Arms of Strangers*, London, November 2000. Nicholas Winton with Prince Charles.

34. Nicholas Winton with Dr Elizabeth Maxwell and Matej Minac at the ICA premiere of *All My Loved Ones*, London, 1999.

My parents' hopes of coming to England came to an abrupt end when war was declared. I well remember the feeling of devastation that overwhelmed me. I don't remember being offered any comfort then, or later. I stayed with my foster family in Sheffield for five years, without ever feeling part of it. Was it because I never detached myself from my parents, or was the option never made available to me?

At just 16, Sue began her nursing training in a London hospital. Her joy and euphoria when the war ended were dashed when she learned that neither her father nor her mother would be returning from the camps.

The effect on me was devastating. In that hospital we slept in open dormitories, there wasn't even anywhere private to cry. I was too stressed to continue with the job and there was no one around to suggest or advise what I should do. I had a boyfriend, then in the Forces, who offered his mother's home in Sheffield, which I gladly accepted. He even paid my fare from London and shared his sergeant's allowance with me when we married.

The past 50 years have certainly helped me to catch up and re-create: three daughters, seven grandchildren and a late, but apparently successful career in education. In 1985 I was awarded an MBE while head of an Inner City Nursery School – work which I loved.

Sue is too modest to mention the true extent of her activities in social and community work. Over the years she fostered 15 babies and adopted one. Since retiring she has continued her voluntary work with the Samaritans, the Children's Information Service, the Sheffield Family Service Unit and Home Start. She also finds time to teach illiterate teenagers to read and to counsel bereaved children. Thirteen years ago Sue helped to set up Holocaust education in schools and continues to talk to pupils and teachers – her one wish is to help bring about the rejection of discrimination.

In November 2000, Sue was awarded an honorary doctorate by Sheffield Hallam University for her outstanding contribution in the field of education. Quite an achievement for someone whose education stopped at the age of 14!

* * *

Eva Leadbeater (née Praeger) is yet another example. Deputy Head of a large comprehensive school, she has taken on, since retirement, work as a volunteer for Oxfam and is an English Language home tutor for immigrants. In her positive way, she expresses her feelings in a few words: 'I have not found fame or fortune; only the good fortune to have been one of Nicky Winton's children, to have enjoyed my work, to be in good health and, not least, to be happily married.'

* * *

John Fieldsend (born Hans Heinrich Feige) spent his early years in Dresden. He came from a mixed background: father German, mother Austro-Czech. John's older brother (who does not wish to be identified) was German and John was German-Czech. They had many gentile friends; they observed Yom Kippur and celebrated Easter and Christmas. John remembers the growing anti-Semitism which drove his father, in the autumn of 1937, to move to his wife's parental home in Vitkov, the Sudetenland, where John had been born.

In the Sudetenland there was no respite from persecution of Jews, particularly after Munich. In late spring 1939 the boys were suddenly told 'You are going to England.' The brothers spent several weeks at a Jewish refugee dispersion centre in Hanover until they joined the *kindertransports* from Prague at the end of June.

My foster-parents, the Cumsty family, were members of the Church of England and were actively Christian. I went to church and Sunday school as a matter of course. They were a wonderful family and I was very happy there. They had

150

one son, seven months older than me, and we got on very well, but we were treated differently, which made me feel a bit of an outsider. This was deliberate on their part, as they did not want to alienate me from my parents. I didn't get the physical attention, but neither the punishment. No hugs – no hidings. There were advantages and disadvantages [John adds, smiling rather sadly].

The Jewish Refugee Committee inspected some foster homes from time to time; in 1943 the Committee was concerned that John was growing up in a devoutly Christian environment. He was transferred from his grammar school to Stoatley Rough School in Hazlemere.

In his book *The Messianic Jews* (Monarch Press, 1993), John vividly describes this period of his life:

When the Jewish Refugee Committee realised what was happening, they felt it necessary to counter the Christian influence on me, but not being able to justify actually removing me from this family, they sent me to a Jewish boarding school. As I was only about 12 years old, who was I to object? I certainly have happy memories of my three years there. I was in a Jewish environment in term time, and back with my Christian foster family in holidays. Just before my barmitzvah I came to the very clear conclusion that what I had been taught about Jesus was true. To cut the story short, I was baptised at St John's Church, Worksop in 1947. Needless to say I was not welcome to return to the boarding school!

When I asked John what drew him to the Christian faith, he replied:

What I saw in the Cumsty home – the warmth, the happiness – the happiest times were always Christmas and Easter. It reminded me so much of my own home and parents [he lost them and most of his relatives in the camps]. The typical response of the Church of the day to

151

my baptism was 'forget that you have been Jewish; put your past behind you' and, for a while, I became more English than the English, more gentile than the gentile. I never forgot that I was Jewish, but something in me died.

John decided at the age of 26 to enter the Church. Whilst at college he came across the Church's Ministry Among the Jewish People and the Hebrew Christian Alliance.

Following his marriage and ordination in 1961, he served in a very Jewish part of Manchester and this was instrumental in rekindling his Jewish identity. But it was not until some years later that, when he was vicar of Christ Church, Bayston Hill, Shrewsbury, the events which were to transform his life began.

John and his wife, Elisabeth, who worked with handicapped children, developed a special ministry amongst people with mental handicaps; over the next 15 years they built a Life Care Home for ten disabled adults; it stands alongside the new church built for the congregation that had grown significantly during John's 22 years as vicar. His natural gift for counselling people led him to attend a course run by Dr Frank Lake on 'The Healing of Memories':

> In a matter of hours I changed from being a student to being a client. I thought I had forgotten and forgiven, but actually I buried the whole lot. At the conference it all erupted. My innate Jewishness burst through the barrier of supressed memory into the vital centre of my being. For the next months I went into an automatic pilot kind of existence and then into what I can describe as a tunnel experience. Entering as a very gentilised Christian, I came out as a Messianic Jew, though for years more I did not use that term, simply because I had not heard of it.

John had a real identity crisis, almost a breakdown, but with the support of Elisabeth and others in his parish, who had the gift and courage to minister to their own minister, the past was relived and healed.

The church rejoiced with me in what the Lord was doing in the life of its own Jewish vicar; they encouraged me not only to explore my roots, but to share my new life with them and to teach them about the Jewish roots of their own faith.

John, now retired, lives with his wife in Oxfordshire; they have two sons and a daughter, all of whom are practising Christians. They have always been interested in the past, one son, David, particularly. When they visited the family home in Vitkov David pronounced: 'Now I know who I am.' He changed his name from Fieldsend back to Feige.[1]

FUELLED BY ADVERSITY

It is incredible how many child refugees, despite adversity, or maybe fuelled by it, made an extraordinary success of their lives and rose to the peak of their professions.

Josef Alon (born Joe Placek) was ten years old when he arrived in England in July 1939 and subsequently went to the Czech school. He was an easy-going, mischievous, exceptionally handsome boy, with a radiant smile. He had no idea that, although he came on a transport from Prague, he was born on a kibbutz in Palestine and that his family, unable to adjust to the harsh conditions prevailing at that time, moved to Czechoslovakia soon after he was born.

After the war, on 27 August 1945, Joe was one of ten children squatting with me on the floor of an RAF bomber – homeward bound at last. We had all dreamed of this moment for so long – of being reunited with our parents, but our dreams had been brutally crushed. We were all orphans and had to face that reality and an uncertain future.

I was luckier than most. My aunt, the sole survivor of my family, was waiting for me, but there was no one waiting for Joe.

I had not seen him for some months when he turned up, unexpectedly, at our tiny flat, hungry, unshaven, grubby and somewhat the worse for drink!

Later, wrapped in my dressing gown, his hunger appeased, he told us his sorry tale. War orphans under the age of 17, with no surviving relatives, had been placed in orphanages or with families. As a borderline case, Joe found himself in a hostel with concentration camp survivors who, like him, had nowhere to go. There he was left, more or less, to fend for himself, living in an atmosphere . which was a constant painful reminder of his parents' suffering. After the happy, friendly atmosphere of our school in Wales, this harsh, postwar adult world was difficult to handle.

Joe stayed with us for a couple of weeks; then he disappeared, without a word, without a trace. Thirty-five years later, when I visited Hugo Marom in Israel, I was told the rest of his story.

Apparently, Joe trained as a silversmith; on the eve of his graduation, he turned up at the lodgings of his friend Hugo Marom, also an orphaned Winton child, who was about to leave the next morning for a pilot's course. He was looking for volunteers in Czechoslovakia to train for the Israeli Air Force. The two young men talked through the night. Just before sunrise, Joe decided to go along with his friend. 'I was never a Zionist – but I wanted to fly.'

Together with Hugo, Ezer Weizman[2] and Motty Hod, Joe was one of the founders of the Israeli Air Force. An outstanding pilot, he trained many of Israel's greatest air commanders and quickly rose through the ranks to become the first squadron commander of the famous Mirage fighters. He reached the peak of his career when he served as commanding officer of the first airbase built from scratch by the IAF – a task in which he took great pride.

Popular with his men, flamboyant, charming and handsome he was every girl's dream; he became a warm family man, devoted to his wife Dvora and their three daughters.

In 1970, Joe was appointed Air Attaché to the Israeli Embassy in Washington. On 1 July 1973, a few weeks before the end of his term of office, Joe was murdered in the driveway of his Washington home. It may have been a random killing; it may have been an act of revenge by terrorists; the case has remained unsolved to this day.

Joe's memory lives on. When I was in Israel with my partner, Harry, a few years ago, we drove from Beersheva along Alon Road, a quiet country lane, to the Joe Alon Centre at Kibbutz Lahav. The centre, which concentrates on archaeology, folklore and nature and on the culture and customs of the Bedouin people, is a fitting memorial to Joe who had always been a lover of nature and of humankind, and a good friend to the Bedouins.

There is a large portrait of Joe above exhibits depicting his brilliant career. Remembering how the odds had been stacked against him when as teenagers we returned to Prague, I felt proud to have known him and terribly sad to have lost such a good friend, who had achieved so much.

Some time later, in a London restaurant, I happened to meet two Israeli pilots. I asked if the name Joe Alon meant anything to them. 'Know him? He taught us all we know. Joe Alon is a legend', was their reply.

How much he would have loved to have shaken Nicky's hand and how proud of him Nicky would have been. After all, Nicky was a pilot too!

* * *

Hugo Marom, who with Joe Alon excelled himself in the War of Independence, was the young boy left stranded at Liverpool Street Station with his brother Rudy and the three Tomaschoff boys.

The parents of the three brothers eventually succeeded in getting into Palestine. Their sons followed when war ended. Felix, the eldest, was killed fighting in the War of Independence, Erwin, the youngest became a prominent lawyer in Chicago but, sadly, died some years ago. The remaining brother, Willi, now known as Aharon Tomaschoff became a district judge (now retired) in Beersheba, Israel.

Hugo and Rudy's parents perished in the camps. Rudy, after a short stay in Czechoslovakia, joined an uncle in the US and lives there still, happily married to his second wife.

Hugo is renowned internationally in the planning and building of airports, the most ambitious being a huge airport over the sea, in Tel Aviv.

He has immense ability, drive, zest for life and compassion for other human beings; to many Israelis he is a household name. But life has not always been easy; not only did he lose both his parents, but tragically a daughter. Whatever knocks in life he or his family may suffer, he is always there for anyone in need of help. He was a great friend and support to Bill Barazetti when Bill was old and frail and had fallen on hard times.

* * *

Tom Berman, a recently retired research professor, is another Winton child who settled in Israel and rose to the peak of his profession. An only child of well-to-do Czech parents, he came to Britain when only five years old – one of the youngest on the transports. To this day, he wonders how his parents found the strength to let him go – at such a tender age.

> I must have been quite traumatised when I arrived in Glasgow in July 1939. I wouldn't let anyone near me for the first few months, but then I acclimatised to my surroundings. I learnt English very quickly and equally quickly forgot my Czech. Mr and Mrs Miller, my foster-parents, had no children of their own and wanted a girl, but were persuaded to take me. They did everything they could to make me happy and settled, but at the same time, they were scrupulous in talking to me about my parents; there was never any doubt that, had they survived, I would have returned to them. I grew up in a loving Jewish household and, until her death in 1996, had a filial relationship with my foster-mother who was an unassuming, caring, saintly woman.
>
> There was never any question of going back to Czechoslovakia. I had become increasinly involved in the Zionist Youth Movement, Habonim, and thus decided that it was much more important to become a 'pioneer' in Israel than a university student in Glasgow. I spent 18 months on a training farm in Berkshire (unknowingly a few miles from the Wintons' home!) and came to Israel in 1952. I have been

a member of Kibbutz Amiad since 1953, with some time off: army service, eight years of study in the US for my degree in Agriculture and a Ph.D. in Microbiology, and a few sabbaticals.

In 1967 Tom was asked to set up the Kinneret Limnological Laboratory on the shores of Lake Kinneret (Sea of Galilee), Israel's only large freshwater lake. In the ensuing years he became internationally known as an expert in the field of limnology – the science of lakes – which entailed years of extensive research, project work and lecturing around the world. He still lives with his wife Debby on Kibbutz Amiad, though their three daughters have settled in the US.

When Nicky and I first met Tom in London in 1989 at the 'Fifty Years On: ROK' (Reunion of Kindertransports), he mentioned how unhappy he was that he was unable to discover anything about his father's family. No relatives, no history – nothing. Some weeks later, Mila, the widow of my mother's cousin came on a visit from Prague. On seeing Tom's name on the list of the children saved and noting his age, she exclaimed 'I knew him as a little boy. His father was a cousin of mine.' This discovery opened the door to Tom's paternal past and led to a warm relationship with Mila and her daughter, who lives in Heidelberg – as well as with myself. Mila, sadly, died two years ago.

Tom says: 'I now identify more or less strongly with three distinguished and historically persecuted minorities – the Jews, the Scots and the Czechs!'

* * *

Fifteen-year-old Hanus Grosz came to Britain in April 1939 with his younger brother, Karl. They were from a professional, well-to-do family in Brno and were accustomed to city life. It was quite a shock to find themselves on an Oxfordshire farm, milking cows and bringing in the harvest. Hanus recalls:

As we spoke no English we felt totally isolated from the local community, even the children, so we were eventually

157

sent to a Zionist agricultural youth camp (Youth Aliyah) which was to prepare us to emigrate to Palestine as pioneers on a kibbutz. We shared the camp life with 60 or so refugee children mainly from Germany and Austria. We worked on surrounding farms and received instruction in Hebrew and Jewish history. Our dreams of going were shattered when Britain put a halt to any further immigration to Palestine.

The brothers then left the camp, Hanus to be apprenticed as a garage mechanic, his brother as a carpenter. Hanus continues:

When I was 18, I joined the RAF, with the Czechoslovak Bomber Squadron. My brother fought in the Czechoslovak Tank Brigade. After the war we met in Prague and found ourselves bereft of family, relatives and childhood friends. My return to the liberated Czechoslovakia was cut short by the impending communist *Putsch* and the consequent threatened arrests (on trumped-up charges) of Czech soldiers and airmen who served with the Allied forces in the West.

Back in Britain, Hanus pursued his dream of becoming a physician, partly to honour his father and partly to serve others. He graduated in 1953 and nine years later emigrated to the US with his Danish wife Kirsten and their three children.

Hanus Grosz became Professor of Psychiatry at the University of Indiana Medical School and certainly made it in life. 'I was idealistic', he said shortly before he died in September 2001, 'and I hope I still am. I also felt that I had a responsibility – that I owed something to the world.'

* * *

Lady Milena Grenfell-Baines (née Fleischmann) is an incredibly energetic, enthusiastic and versatile Winton child with a wide range of interests and a strong organising ability.

Prior to the German occupation of Czechoslovakia, Milena's

father, an active social democrat and an MP, had been involved in helping political enemies of the Third Reich (such as the German author, Thomas Mann) reach safety and thus had placed himself and his family in danger. Happily, he managed to escape and made his way to England a day before the Germans marched in.

Ten-year-old Milena, her five-year-old sister Eva and cousin Helena followed him to England at the end of June. Incredibly, Milena's mother, a doctor of Latvian origin, escaped via Norway as late as 1940; Helena's parents also managed to reach England.

Milena realised how lucky she was only in 1941 when she joined the Czech school. 'My family were reunited; most of the children had come without their parents. I didn't know then that they would never see them again.'

After the war the family decided to remain in Preston. Milena trained and worked as a nanny; anxious to prove to her disapproving father that she was no cabbage, she accepted a post as governess in France and returned to Preston fluent in French. In 1954 she married George Grenfell-Baines, one of Britain's foremost architects and founder of the Building Design Partnership, who was knighted for his services to architecture.

Despite the stringent, hardline, communist regime of the early 1960s, Milena's husband, prompted by her attachment and affection for her homeland, established links with Czechoslovakia through the Society of Architects. He lectured in Prague and set up an exchange system through which Czech architects and students were given the opportunity to gain experience in his offices. Milena came into her own as hostess and interpreter.

The extensive entertaining required by her husband's position inspired Milena to run cookery courses, organise foreign cookery weeks in Preston and abroad – even a banquet in Nimes! – as well as various charity events.

Milena's interests and activities also embrace the world of music. More than 20 years ago she founded the Friends of the Liverpool Philharmonic Society (in Preston) and has been raising funds and performing many other duties ever since. She organises and accompanies tours to the continent, mainly to the Czech Republic, for the orchestra and for the Friends. In 1990 the

Liverpool Philharmonic was privileged to open Prague's annual music festival – the first festival after the 1989 Velvet Revolution and the first time a foreign orchestra gave the opening concert for the Prague Spring. The bond between the two countries was strengthened further when Libor Pesek, the Czech conductor, became Principal Conductor and Musical Director of the Liverpool Philharmonic from 1987 to 1997.

For several years Milena was the Chairman of the British Czech and Slovak Association (BCSA), founded in the period of the 1989 euphoria. The association, *inter alia*, promotes cultural, educational and business links between Milena's former and present homes. Her horizons are forever widening; both she and Sir George are household names throughout Preston and greatly respected and loved by all who know them.

In 1999, Milena received Jan Masaryk's Gratias Agit award for her many years of endeavour to promote the bonds between the two countries closest to her heart – an honour she has rightly earned.

Milena's sister Eva married an architect who worked in Sir George's office and eventually they emigrated to the US.

Cousin Helena returned to Prague with her parents after the war; under the communists they suffered great hardships. Her father, who had served in the Royal Air Force and fought for the freedom of his country, was imprisoned; Helena and her mother were thrown out of their apartment. Many Czech ex-servicemen who had fought at the side of the British were placed in cells – ironically with German war criminals – and this by their own people, not by the enemy!

* * *

Lord Alf Dubs was already bilingual when he arrived in Britain as a seven-year-old – his father was Czech, his mother Austrian. He was luckier than most, for his parents managed to follow him, but tragically his father died soon after reaching freedom. Alf grew up in Manchester where his mother found work, but spent the last two years of the war in the Czech school. When war ended, his mother decided not to return to Prague; most of their relatives and friends had been murdered; those who had survived soon left to start life again elsewhere. She was also apprehensive of the growing strength of communism.

Politics had interested Alf from an early age. At the time of the 1945 general election he was only 13 years old, but he followed the events with a passionate interest. A keen supporter of the Labour Party, he was ecstatic when they won by a large majority.

After National Service, Alf attended the London School of Economics and as soon as he was old enough, joined the Labour Party. In 1979 he was elected to Parliament for Battersea South and was Member for Battersea until 1987; he was Home Affairs frontbencher and Shadow Minister for Police, Prisons and Criminal Justice.

During his political career Alf held many posts: for several years he was, most appropriately, Director of the Refugee Council and, to this day, is Deputy Chair of the Broadcasting Standards Commission; he also served as an elected Councillor on Westminster City Council, on an Area Health Authority, a Mental Hospital Trust, held the Chair of the Fabian Society, of Liberty and of Westminster Community Relations Council; he was a Trustee of Action Aid and served on committees of a number of other voluntary organisations.

Politics have been Alf's life, particularly work connected with human rights. In 1994 he was made a Labour working peer. After Labour's election victory in 1997 he was appointed Parliamentary Under-Secretary of State for Northern Ireland, a post he held until December 1999. Currently he is Chair of the Labour Party in the Lords. Alf is modest to the extreme and embarrassed when questioned about his work. He considers his life to have been very ordinary, even dull. But those of us who knew him as a young boy and renewed contact in later years are justly proud of our former schoolmate, as is Nicky, who does not like to miss any opportunity of seeing him.

A very special occasion was their meeting on 14 June 1999 in the Palace of Westminster, when, standing side by side, Nicky the rescuer and Alf whom he had saved, watched together as Betty Boothroyd, Speaker of the House, unveiled a plaque which reads:

IN DEEP GRATITUDE
TO THE PEOPLE AND PARLIAMENT
OF THE UNITED KINGDOM
FOR SAVING THE LIVES OF
10,000 JEWISH AND OTHER CHILDREN
WHO FLED TO THIS COUNTRY
FROM NAZI PERSECUTION
ON THE KINDERTRANSPORT
1938–1939

COMING HOME

As we have seen, many of the orphaned Winton children, devastated by the loss of their families, chose not to return to Czechoslovakia when hostilities ceased. This applied particularly to the younger ones who had forgotten their mother tongue and felt estranged from the country of their birth. They clung to the life they had established in Britain – relationships forged with foster-parents, sweethearts, friends, the security of living amongst people and under conditions which had become far more familiar than the distant past. Life would have turned out differently had there been someone to go back to.

The situation for the children at the Czech School was different. We looked upon Britain as our second home, felt part of the community and, in most cases, remain strongly attached to the families who had taken us into their homes, yet I cannot recall anyone at that time who wanted to remain in Britain. We had kept our language and customs, we were up to date in education and immersed in Czech culture. And we were so patriotic! Whatever awaited us, we were determined to return to help rebuild our country and endeavour to find out what had happened to family and friends. The future of those few pupils whose parents had managed to escape was decided for them. The rest of us were now orphans. Some had a relative, however distant, who survived the camps or had escaped to the West and now offered a home; the remainder became the responsibility of the Czechoslovak state. The future was decided for us: we would be repatriated as soon as possible. I doubt that anyone minded. As much as we were dazed and grieved by the blow that fate had dealt us, we were eager to return to our country where we felt we belonged. Thus, during July and August 1945 several groups of young refugees were repatriated in RAF planes bound for Prague. It was a sad homecoming.

The German *kinder* were in a more difficult position. How could they consider returning to their homeland when it was their own countrymen who had murdered their families? In our case the enemy was the murderer. We were apprehensive about our uncertain future, but had high hopes of being welcomed.

* * *

When Alice Klimova (née Justitzova) returned to Prague in August 1945 she knew that her sister would be waiting for her. In a way, she owed her life to Mimka; back in the spring of 1939 a family had been found through the Woodcraft Folk for Mimka, but as she was over the age limit, 11-year-old Alice, at the last minute, took her place. Fortunately, Mimka managed to obtain a permit to train in London as a nurse and left on a later transport as one of the carers.

Alice's first foster-parents, a young couple with a baby, were kind and considerate, but when the husband was called up, money was short and another baby was on the way. Alice then moved on, to a middle-aged childless Christian couple, then to the home of elderly orthodox Jews: 'They were kind and well-meaning', Alice remembers, 'but I had been brought up in a non-religious household. Their way of life was foreign to me. I tried to stick to their ways, hoping that all that praying would help save my parents.' Ultimately Alice lived with her sister in London until she happily joined the Czech School.

Mimka left England as soon as war ended; by then she was married to a Czech soldier and was pregnant. As a qualified nurse she joined the Red Cross and was one of the first to reach the ghetto town of Terezin, where conditions were appalling and disease was rife. She was able to help the survivors and comfort the dying. By the time Alice was repatriated in August Mimka, back in Prague, was waiting for her at the airport. Alice recalls:

> She came every day, not knowing when I would arrive, so she wouldn't miss me. We had nowhere to live and for months moved from place to place before we found a tiny flat. Mimka and her husband took it for granted that I would live with them. She was mother and sister all in one – and I took her love for granted. Looking back, I don't know how I would have coped with life without her.

In 1948, after qualifying as a teacher, Alice married Bob Klíma, who had also escaped to Britain and joined the Czech division of the British Army. On his return to Prague he worked at the Ministry of Foreign Trade, but was thrown out in 1951 by the communists. As he was *persona non grata*, having served in the British forces, they were forced to move, with their baby son, to a small provincial town, where they spent the next 15 tough, unhappy years. In 1966, the political situation eased and they were permitted to return to Prague. Life still had its problems, but 'I decided my home is where my roots are – and up to a point everywhere where my good friends from the Czech School are. They are my family.'

Alice did not consciously choose to marry a Jew, but is sure this contributed to her happiness and understanding and kept her safe and stable through the difficult years. Bob died in 1983.

Alice and I have become very close; we are like sisters. In June 1988, I went to Prague with the video featuring the Winton story as shown on the Esther Rantzen programme, which had had such an impact on TV audiences in the UK earlier that year. Alice's daughter, Vera, and 11-year-old grandson, were moved to tears. The visual details of the events of those days made the young mother and son realise what turmoil parents and children must have suffered before being torn apart forever.

* * *

Eleven-year-old Joe Schlesinger and his nine-year-old brother, Ernie, who lived in Bratislava, the capital of Slovakia, were due to leave for Britain at the end of June 1939. As Slovakia was an autonomous state they could travel through the protectorate only on a transit visa. Arrangements had, therefore, been made for the boys to join the *kindertransport* from Prague at Lovositz, the first station inside Nazi Germany. There, the station guard informed their father, who had travelled with them, that the train had been delayed and would not arrive until the following morning. It was suggested, quite politely, that they were welcome to spend the night in the toilets; for Jews, waiting rooms were out of bounds. 'The smell of tar-coated urinals bring back the night at Lovositz. The feeling is not of humiliation, but of warmth, of comfort, and drowsy contentment, as my father quietly talked to me', Joe writes in his autobiography *Time Zones* (Random House, Toronto, 1990).

> As I have watched my children grow past the age I was then, my mind has gnawed at what must have been going through his head as he sat there, waiting to send his children off on a journey that would take them to safety, but also to a world where he could not follow and where his sons might remain lost to him forever.

That was the last time Joe and Ernie saw their father.

In England each boy went to live with a different uncle, where they were given an indifferent welcome. Joe was shuffled from one foster home to another until he came to the Czech School, where Ernie later joined him.

After the war, with no news of their parents' survival and no attempts by their uncles to persuade them to stay in the UK, they became part of the group of war orphans ferried back to Prague in an RAF plane.

In Prague there was no one who cared about their future. They were just a couple of boys amongst the thousands of displaced and dispossessed. At first, they were placed in a hostel. Eventually Ernie ended up in an orphanage where he was desperately unhappy and worried about his future, until he heard of a scheme under which Jewish orphans could emigrate to Canada. He never looked back.

In the meantime Major Rakous, a Catholic, gave Joe a home. This gesture was not prompted by compassion, nor by generosity, but by the Major's desire for a larger apartment. Accommodation was almost impossible to come by; Joe would increase the Major's family to six thereby enabling him to claim a more spacious flat.

Neither survivors nor returning refugees could get their homes back; possession was almost law. My aunt, a survivor of Auschwitz and Belsen, pleaded with the Housing Authority for over a year before they gave in and allocated us the smallest room, the tiny kitchen and the use of the toilet in what had been her flat. The rest of the spacious accommodation which still housed her own furniture, remained permanently in the possession of the local butcher and his family who had moved in immediately after she and my grandfather were deported.

This was a common situation. When Joe and Ernie visited their home in the town of Bratislava, the strangers now living there did not allow the brothers to enter. Their late father's Aryan partner swore that their family store was now legally his. The boys fought for the return of the business and eventually won – I faced the same problem but lost, as did many others.

We were trying to get our lives back. We knew it would not be easy, but we did not expect such lack of compassion, such hostility from our own people, even from family friends. This was extremely painful; there were some who welcomed us with open arms, spontaneously returning possessions left with them by our parents. Others brazenly denied that they had been entrusted with anything of value. We all learnt to expect and to dread the look which spelt out wordlessly 'Why did *my* Jew have to return?'.

* * *

On our return to Prague, Joe and Hanus Snabl (see page 114), my old classmates from Wales, joined the same gymnasium (grammar school) as I did. We were 17 and wished to complete our secondary education, which proved something of an ordeal. Our fellow pupils eyed us with undisguised, less than friendly, curiosity. 'I thought Hitler got you all', one of them sniggered. Not only the pupils, but some teachers, showed cold indifference, even envy, that we had been in Britain whilst they were suffering under the Nazi occupation. That we had lost our families and homes was of no consequence. We were not accepted, but treated as outsiders because we were Jewish. Joe and Hanus eventually changed schools, but I stuck it out until I passed my matriculation.

Hanus' homecoming was particularly sad as he had not only lost his parents, but his brother. Franta should have left for Britain with my two cousins and 247 other children on the transport dramatically prevented from leaving by the declaration of war. These negative experiences were just a foretaste of what was to come. Gradually, with the growing strength of communism all hopes and illusions of freedom and democracy were dashed; this culminated in February 1948 when President Eduard Benes was forced to surrender our country to the communists without a fight.

At that time Joe was recovering from a major problem unconnected with politics. In spring 1946 tuberculosis was diagnosed in his hip joint and he spent the next two years being shuffled between various hospitals and sanatoria.

Unaware of what was happening to Joe, I was working as head of a translating pool at the Ministry of Defence. Towards the end of 1947 I chose to ignore the volatile political climate, naively confident that no drastic change would take place; I accepted the post, tempted by the promise that within a year I would be working as secretary to the Military Attaché at the Czechoslovak Embassy in London. I missed England, my English family, but most of all my sister who had decided to remain there. With such a job I would have the best of both worlds.

My optimism was short lived. Communism brought dictatorship, fear, distrust and purges. At the Ministry many officers and other high-level employees, who had returned from the West, simply disappeared. Rumours were rife of dismissals, arrests and imprisonment; my turn came when there was a leakage of confidential military information to which I had access. This, coupled with my undesirable background and anti-communist views, made me a prime suspect. I was interrogated at the Ministry for two days and two nights and would have been banished to Siberia, on the grounds of suspicion only, had they not discovered the real culprit. Flight Lieutenant Eddie Simon, head of my department, had become my good friend and was advising me how to keep out of trouble; yet he was playing with fire. Alas, after years of imprisonment, Eddie was shot for treason.

I knew then that I had to get away, but the thought of leaving my aunt, whom I loved dearly, haunted me. She had been at my mother's side throughout the four nightmare years in the camps, ending in Belsen where Mother died in her arms. Aunt Berta also buried Tommy and Honza, my cousins who almost made it to Britain. All three died of typhus a few days after the end of the war.

With the Iron Curtain separating us, I knew it would be a very long time before my aunt and I would meet again – if ever. But I dared not stay. I gave in my notice and concentrated on getting a passport – an impossible task, everyone told me. It took a year of persistent effort, determination and much bribery, but I got it in the end.

I returned to Britain in January 1949 determined to put the past behind me, but have never lost the love for my country. In the summer of that year I met Michael Gissing, a young Englishman; we later married and soon started a family. At last I had roots, a new beginning! There was no point in pining for my old home, my aunt and my friends. For them contact with the West was strictly forbidden; letters were censored, personal visits out of the question. A few innocent lines, a careless phone-call could brand a person an enemy of the state which could result in severe punishment.

Aunt Berta took no notice of such directives. She was careful what she said, but she never stopped writing and neither did I, knowing that my letters were her lifeline. After her retirement she was allowed to visit us, but she refused to make her home with us. She always brought news of Alice and other friends, but never a word about Joe or Hanus.

When, in 1964, Hanus came on an official visit to the London Motor Show, I was horrified to learn that a year after I left, he was arrested and imprisoned and later sent to dig tunnels in the mines. Almost worked to death and on a starvation diet, he suffered great hardship for seven and a half years. His crime? He simply did not fit the format demanded by the communists and thus was considered an enemy of the regime. When eventually he was pardoned, he found work as editor of a motor magazine in Prague which gave him the opportunity to come to the Motor Show in London where he remained. Until his retirement Hanus worked for the Czech Section of the BBC World Service, where he met his wife, Tania, who worked for the Slovak Section – a happy Czech and Slovak union!

Hanus had heard disturbing rumours that Joe had been shot whilst trying to escape across the border, maybe even killed.

The following summer, as Hanus was driving late at night from my home in Hemel Hempstead towards the motorway, he was flagged down by a young man desperate to get to London. Glad of the company, he gave him a lift. His passenger mentioned that he was on his way to Paris for a job interview with the New York *Herald Tribune*, European edition. On parting they exchanged visiting cards.

He did not get the job, but he did have dinner with the assistant managing editor; over coffee his host mentioned that originally he came from Czechoslovakia. 'What a coincidence; I was given a lift by a Czech only last night', the young man said and fished the visiting card out of his pocket. The unbelievable had happened. The man's host was Joe Schlesinger – very much alive – fit and well, with a wife and two daughters and most anxious to see us. Hanus drove to Paris the very next day.

When we met soon afterwards in London, I learnt that when Joe finally regained his health, he worked as a translator and interpreter for the American Bureau at the Czechoslovak News Agency (CTK), hoping that the Americans would help to get him out of the country. Joe soon realised that there was no chance of obtaining a passport and that he would have to try to escape illegally. After one unsuccessful attempt in December 1949, he tried again, the following February. With his then girlfriend, Helena, Joe made his way to a small town in southern Moravia, which was separated from the Austrian border by a solidly frozen river. To avoid suspicion they strolled on the river bank, pretending to be lovers. Then on a count of three, they separated, turned and ran across the river. 'On the other side, we ran up the bank and flopped into the snow beyond it. We just lay there rolling in the snow with happiness. We had necked our way through the Iron Curtain', Joe recalls in his autobiography.

Joe made his way to Canada, to the Pacific Ocean, where he worked on a passenger ship as mess boy, which helped him to recover from the traumatic years spent in and out of hospitals, wondering if he would ever walk again and later if he would succeed in giving the communists the slip or end up in jail.

After a year Joe enrolled at the University of British Columbia to study economics. He joined the campus newspaper *The Ubyssey* and also contributed to major Canadian newspapers in Toronto and Vancouver. These were the first firm steps in his journalist career which, in 1962, brought him to Paris.

Paris will always remain a magical city to Joe. There he met his wife, Mike, an American, working for the US Foreign Service. Their two daughters were born in Paris and the four years spent there were filled with the love and happiness that had eluded him for so long. Mike died in 2001.

Canada, however, was to be their permanent home. Joe returned there with his new family and soon established himself as an internationally known, highly respected and accomplished journalist. He joined CBC Television News as Executive Producer of the National and as Head of Television News. For 21 years Joe worked as their foreign correpondent in Hong Kong, Paris, Washington and Berlin. He has received three Gemini Awards for his documentaries on the Spanish Civil War, his coverage of the Iran-Contra affair and for his reporting on the Gulf War in 1991. Joe was also named Member of the Order of Canada in 1995. After working for three years as Chief Political Correspondent, Joe retired, but to this day he continues to contribute to CBC TV News as special correspondent; he also hosts his own weekly half-hour programme on foreign affairs on Newsworld.

* * *

There are many more tales to tell about Nicky Winton's children; it has been difficult to decide which stories to include and which to leave out. Every account deserves to be told and it is hard to do justice to individual people in a few paragraphs or pages. I could only do my best.

There are similarities and differences in our wartime experiences and in the way we coped and tackled life afterwards, facing the future alone, bereft of parents and extended family. Whether we have been successful in our lives and careers, or whether we have led humdrum lives is not of prime importance; that we had cheated Hitler, that we were able to rebuild our lives is an achievement, a victory in itself.

Until Nicky entered our lives we did not realise the full extent of our good fortune; almost 5,000 endangered children remained unplaced on Winton's list; they did not make it to Britain. We were the lucky few for whom homes were found before it was too late.

NOTES

1. In later years, John became the UK Director of CMJ (Church's Ministry among the Jewish People) and lived in St Albans. The aim of the Ministry is education in three objectives:

   1. the study of the Jewish roots of the Christian Church;
   2. to encourage Jewish people to maintain their Jewish identity;
   3. to share the faith that Jesus is the Jewish Messiah.

2. Ezer Weizman, nephew of the first President of the State of Israel. After a distinguished career in the RAF and the Israeli Air Force, he entered politics and became a Member of the Knesset (Israeli Parliament). President of the State, 1993–2000.

4 *The Twilight Years*

RETIREMENT

Until the story of his rescue hit the headlines, Nicky's life in retirement had been orderly, peaceful, yet busy. Almost in his eightieth year, he would have been entitled, indeed expected, to take life easy: to potter in his beautiful garden or take a dip in the old unheated pool. His fine physique and agility, his quick mind and sharp wit belied his years. He devoted much of his time to charity work. Weekly meetings at the Rotary Club, his ongoing involvement in Mencap and Abbeyfield Housing Association were (and continue to be) areas in which his help and expertise is constantly needed and willingly given. He now had time for his many hobbies, most of which he shared with his late wife, Grete: theatre, music, particularly opera, bridge, travel. His tapestry work, which he finds most therapeutic, is of a professional standard and adorns his home. The Wintons always led a full and interesting social life with a large circle of friends. Children, grandchildren and other relatives have always played an important part in their lives. Their warm hospitality and Grete's excellent dinners were enjoyed by friends and family alike. Their diary was always full. Yet, from 1988, Nicky always found time for us, his ever-growing extended family.

Strangers would appear at his door, bearing the names that matched those on his list, eager to meet the man who was instrumental in their rescue. He was inundated with invitations to their homes and requests to visit him. For 50 years, a vital piece was missing from the jigsaw puzzle that made up our lives. Now, at last, it could be slotted into its rightful place.

Nicky's compassionate nature and friendly manner and his genuine interest in our lives put everyone at ease and led to many close, affectionate relationships. Grete always welcomed us and made us feel at home. She never forgot a face, or a name; her unobtrusive, quiet manner and friendliness endeared her to all who met her.

As I live only a few miles from the Winton home, we meet frequently. Sometimes Nicky, often with Grete and some of his children, would join me for lunch in my cottage; at other times we got together at their house. My sister Eva, who paid me a surprise visit from New Zealand, was the first of many visitors I was to bring to their home. Her decision to make the journey was prompted by the opportunity to meet Nicky and his children during the 'Remembering for the Future' conference which took place in 1988. Shortly after that event, I was able to present Nicky with the first copy of *Pearls of Childhood*. Without his swift and timely intervention I would not have been here to tell the tale.

One of the most touching moments of that summer occurred when I introduced Nicky to my English foster-mother, Mummy Rainford. She has always been a much-loved member of my family who figured prominently in my early years.

As Nicky and Mummy Rainford shook hands, they said, simultaneously, 'Thank you for Vera'. I hugged them both, as they stood, smiling at each other, in my garden. It was a beautiful day. My granddaughter was playing on the lawn. Nicola, my daughter, sat in the shade, nursing her new baby. The garden was filled with bright flowers, white butterflies and the sound of birds. 'Thank you for all this', I said, brushing the tears from my eyes. 'If it wasn't for you two, I wouldn't be here. I wouldn't have children and grandchildren, nor a cottage and a garden.' I have never felt so rich.

When, in 1939, Mummy Rainford came to fetch me, her first words were 'You shall be loved' – and loved I was. These are the most important words any refugee child, separated from home and family, could hear. A devout Methodist, she was the first female lay preacher in Lancashire. She lived her religion, every day of her life, in giving and caring for the needs of others. She made me realise how important it is to help those less fortunate than oneself. I became familiar with the religious routine within her home and attended church with the family, but never once did she attempt to persuade me that her way would be preferable to the Judaism to which I had been born (my sister and I were, in fact, baptised some months prior to the German occupation; our parents hoping this would protect us).

In the autumn of her life, Mummy Rainford came every summer with her daughter Dorothy to stay in my cottage. On arrival, she always aimed for her favourite chair, facing the garden, and she would say, every time, her warm smile lighting up her face, 'Now I am in heaven.' And now she really is in heaven. She died, peacefully in her sleep, at the age of 103, happy to have seen the birth of the new millennium.

LIFE GATHERS PACE

In May 1989 Nicky and Grete visited Israel for the first time. Financed and arranged by the Maxwells, their journey was made in order to lodge the original records of the rescue mission at Yad Vashem (The Holocaust Martyrs' and Heroes' Remembrance Authority), in Jerusalem.

The Wintons were taken on a guided tour and were deeply moved by what they saw – nothing touched them as much as the memorial to the children who had perished in the Holocaust: in a windowless, silent hall, with one ever-burning light (*ne'ertamid*) and thousands of flickering lights like stars in the darkest sky, a sombre voice calls out name after name – of all the 1.5 million young victims. After such an emotionally stirring experience it was almost a relief to walk through the Avenue of the Righteous Gentiles, where every tree planted honours a non-Jew who, at great risk to his own family, had helped to save Jewish lives. When it was suggested that a tree be planted in Nicky's name, he protested. 'I was taken aback', he told me on his return. 'There were no heroics in what I did and I had a lot of help.'

The opportunity to meet several of the Israeli 'children' was a much happier event, when Hugo Marom gave a festive luncheon in Nicky's honour.

Among those present were Amos Ben Ron (Petr Brunner) and his late wife Gabby (Guns) – as far as I know, the only two Winton children to marry. Amos came to England with his younger brother, Tommy; Gabby with three siblings. Her father, a rabbi, escaped the Nazis and made his way to Palestine, but her mother perished. Amos' parents, after their son's departure, managed to generate sufficient funds to bribe the Nazis to let them go, and to satisfy the conditions stipulated by the British White Paper of 1939 allowing entry into Palestine to married but childless couples of means.

Only days after returning home, Nicky had a big garden party to celebrate his eightieth birthday. 'I'd like you to come', he said to me, 'to represent the children – and bring Harry along, because I like him.'

My husband and I had divorced in 1984, but remained on friendly terms until his death in September 1995. By the time Nicky came on the scene, I was sharing my life with Harry Steinhauer who had been in my class at the Czech School in Wales all those years ago. He is not a Winton child as he left Prague in January 1939, before Nicky's transports got going, but on the day of his departure Nicky was at Prague Airport to see him off with a planeload of children – all destined for the Barbican Mission. Harry was lucky; his parents and sister followed him to England.

As Harry and I mingled with family and friends he remarked that he thought it probable that Nicky was Jewish. 'Don't be silly', I snapped, 'he looks the perfect English gentleman. There's nothing Jewish about him.' As it happened, one of Nicky's old friends, unwittingly settled the matter: 'Did you know his mother, Barbara? A brilliant woman; intelligent, outspoken, quite difficult – didn't tolerate fools gladly. She was a German Jew, originally. She adored Nicky.' Harry and I decided to keep what we had learnt to ourselves.

Towards the end of that year, Nicky received a letter from Hugo Marom, stating that he wished to recommend him to be

Jerusalem, 12th September, 1994

Mr. Nicholas Winton,
New Ditton,
Pinkneys Green,
Maidenhead,
U.K.

Dear Mr. Winton,

Not many of us can look back on saving hundreds of human lives
almost single-handed. And special, even historic significance
is attached to that achievement when those saved were threatened
by the vast war machine of the hostile Nazi regime. In the darkness enveloping Europe in 1939 your selfless dedication to the
salvation of children in Prague shines out.

A half century later 664 adults throughout the world, very many
of them in Israel, know the years they have lived since 1939
were your gift to them - the gift of the young Englishman who
took it upon himself to arrange for their admittance to England
and all the myriad details involved in transporting them there
between March and August 1939. There are volumes in the simple
fact that an additional transport organized for hundreds of
children to leave on September 1 was cancelled with the start
of the War and not a single child survived.

In remembering your role and thanking you for what you did I
speak for all of us in Israel who cherish the tiny remnant of
our people that were saved out of mass death and helped to build
a new life for themselves and others. Your name is written
large on that page of history.

With good wishes to you,

                                Yours sincerely,

                                Ezer Weizman

recognised by Israel as a Righteous Gentile. Nicky replied:

> I can't possibly accept. My contribution was far too modest and my life was never in danger. Besides, Mother and my paternal grandparents were German Jews. My parents were baptised; I was baptised and later confirmed; I've never practised any religion. In fact, I am an agnostic. I certainly didn't consider myself Jewish, but since meeting you children and going to Yad Vashem, I sometimes wonder what I really am, but I suppose, in the eyes of Yad Vashem, I am a Jew ...

Although the honour of qualifying as a Righteous Gentile eluded him, Nicky received a much appreciated letter of thanks from the then President of Israel, Ezer Weizman (see page 170).

DAWN OF A NEW ERA

In June 1989 Nicky met more of his children who had travelled to London from various parts of Britain, the United States and Israel to participate in the International Reunion of the Kindertransport (ROK), to celebrate the fiftieth anniversary of our arrival in Britain. The two-day event was the brainchild of Bertha Leverton – a *kind* who was born in Germany. What began as an idea for a small get-together turned into a gathering of more than 1,000 former child refugees, mostly of German origin, some with husbands and children, who came from all over the world. The Czechs were a small minority, but then almost 10,000 German and Austrian *kinder* had been saved, as opposed to 669 Winton children. The Prague transports had not been part of the *kindertransport* movement as Nicky had to work independently, under stricter rules and regulations. Nevertheless, all of us who were present owed our lives to the kindness of the British people – and that is a very strong bond. To many, who until then had no group with which to identify, the reunion was particularly meaningful.

Nicky listened and spoke to the newcomers with patience and interest; he responded to their gratitude and the attention of the media with his usual modesty. 'I am trying to play the whole thing down as much as I can – it didn't need any particular genius to do what I did. It is nice to find so many children who have done so well.' Then he added, as if the thought had just struck him, 'Perhaps they are the only ones who would come to these events.'

The story of Alice Masters (Eberstark), who came to the reunion from the US with her husband, had the greatest impact on me; it illustrated, so clearly, the terrible dilemma our parents had faced – whether to keep us, or let us go. Alice is still haunted by the memory of the narrow escape she and her two sisters had, particularly her youngest one, Elli. As their train was about to leave Prague station, three times their distraught mother reached in through the compartment window and pulled Elli out – and three times she reluctantly put her back ...

* * *

In 1989 truly momentous events were taking place in Europe. Communist governments were crumbling, revolts and radical reforms were sweeping like bush fires through Poland, Hungary, East Germany and Bulgaria. Would Czechoslovakia be next? I kept wondering as I remembered my country's previous attempt in 1968, when Alexander Dubcek, the Secretary of the Czechoslovak Communist Party had endeavoured to give socialism a human face. It was then – after more than 20 years – that I had dared to return to my homeland with my husband for a brief visit. The world called it the 'Prague Spring' – the spring of hope, unity and renewed national pride.

After two decades of enforced silence the reunion with my old friends, mostly Nicky's children, was highly emotional. My old resolve to put the past behind me soon came crashing down; I felt at one with them – so much at home.

Back in Britain as spring turned into summer, I was commissioned by the BBC's *Woman's Hour* to prepare a programme on the Czech women's hopes for a freer future. I flew to Prague, with my daughters – seven-year-old Sally and her older sister Nicola. Ironically I had timed our arrival for the middle of August – just ahead of the invading Russian tanks. Fearing for the children's safety I felt we had to try to get back to Britain as quickly as possible. In the centre of Prague the evidence of recent clashes was there for all to see: smouldering buildings, overturned cars and trams, burnt-out, abandoned tanks, a mass of people, their ashen faces stained with tears, notices nailed to walls and trees saying 'Russians go home – we don't want you here!'

I felt as if I was reliving the events of March 1939. As if reading my thoughts, Nicola, who had developed an almost instant affinity with the country and the people, gently placed her hand in mine. 'I know now how you must have felt when you watched the Germans march into your town. I am eleven, like you were then', she said. Little Sally added: 'Can we go home? This isn't a happy place any more.'

Twenty years on, in the middle of November 1989, Joe Schlesinger telephoned from Washington. 'I've been asked to cover the Malta Conference', he said, 'but first I want to spend a few days in Prague. I intend to fly back home via London so I can meet up with you and Harry and, most importantly, with Nicky Winton.'

Joe never made it to Malta or to London. His arrival in Prague coincided with the first stirrings of the uprising and, as events gathered momentum, Prague became Joe's priority. He remained there throughout the euphoric days of the Velvet Revolution. Slovak-born and a foreign correspondent, Joe was doubly thrilled to witness the disintegration of communism and the dawn of a new democratic era. He finally met the Wintons at my home the following spring. It was the first of many meetings and there was much to talk about.

* * *

In June 1990 a second reunion of the Czech School was held in the Abernant Hotel, our wartime home in Llanwrtyd Wells. Foreign travel was now possible and several former pupils living in Czechoslovakia were able to attend. Grete and Nicky were honorary guests and they not only won the hearts of the 30 or more of 'his' children, but were 'adopted' by the whole school.

The communist system was no longer there to thwart our efforts and the time was ripe to bring Nicky and his story to the attention of the people in Czechoslovakia and to make the authorities aware of his achievement. It took almost a year to set it up.

In May 1991, more than five decades after his first fateful visit, Nicky returned to Prague with Grete, for what he thought was to be a private holiday. He was unaware that Czechoslovakia, somewhat belatedly, wished to show her gratitude for his remarkable deed. On arrival, he was greeted by his Czech-based children with armfuls of flowers and by representatives of *Lidove noviny* (the national newspaper) and the Jewish community, who jointly insisted that the Wintons would be their guests. Instead of staying with one of the children, as they expected, they were booked into Hotel Evropa, former Hotel Sroubek, where our story began.

I was able to participate in most of the private and official events, which included meetings with 'his' children, visits to the ancient Jewish Quarter – the synagogues, the museum, the famous cemetery. We were all moved at the festive lunch by the words of Mr Danicek, the Head of the Jewish Community, who said to Nicky: 'I want to thank you twice, as a Czech and as a Jew, for saving so many of our children.' We were equally proud of our rescuer when, in the Old Town Hall, the mayor, Mr Koran, granted him the Freedom of the City. President Vaclav Havel also wished to extend his personal thanks and he received the Wintons at Hradcany Castle. Their 12-day stay ended with an informal lunch at the National Assembly, presided over by Alexander Dubcek, Speaker of the House. This veteran reformer, whose attempts to give communism a human face were brutally crushed in 1968, and Nicky found many topics of conversation in common. Tragically he was killed in a car crash 18 months later.

Nicky handled this tiring programme calmly without losing patience with the reporters who pestered him daily. When asked what pleased him most during his stay, he did not refer to the honours and the acclaim he had received, but replied unhesitatingly, as he always does, 'To see all the children doing well – being glad to be alive.'

SERVICE ABOVE SELF

Nicky, a very private man, tries his hardest to conceal his feelings, but his outward reserve is just a mask hiding a compassionate, emotional man. He is often visibly shaken on hearing of the tragic losses and tough times his children had suffered in their youth. When he hears, time and time again, how, almost without exception, they had lost their parents and identity, he grieves with them; when told how they rebuilt their lives, of their successes and happiness in later years, his relief and pleasure is there for all to see.

In his long life, saving the children (which covered a period of only nine months) has come to be recognised as the most important single deed of all his humanitarian acitivites, but he is also admired and respected for his continuous services to the community for which he was awarded an MBE in the Queen's Honours in 1983.

Winton House, the Abbeyfield Extra Care Home in Windsor, Nicky's pride and joy, was opened in 1984 and considerably extended in 1991. His dedication, drive and ability have resulted in the overall success of the home. As a much respected and an acknowledged expert on Extra Care, Nicky's advice has been an inspiration to others throughout the Abbeyfield movement. I have seen for myself how his presence affects the staff and residents – how they brighten at the very sight of him. It is not just a place for the old folk to spend their last years – Nicky has seen to it that it has the feel and the comforts of a real home.

This applies also to his involvement in Mencap. A few years ago, Nicky, who remains president of the local branch, invited Harry and me to their club, where members of the borough gather once a month. He was aware that we were both on the UK national committee of Akim, a Jewish charity which cares for Israel's mentally and physically handicapped, particularly children. What followed was a revelation: the moment he entered, children and adults alike flocked to his side, surrounding him as if he was their Pied Piper, shouting 'Nicky, Nicky's here', fighting to hug him, clutch his hand or just to hang onto his sleeve. He knew them all by name and had a kind word for everyone. I shall never forget the look of devotion in their eyes, nor his patience and gentleness. At no time was his genuine concern for his fellow human beings so touchingly displayed as on that, to me, most meaningful occasion, which reconfirmed, once again, that Nicky not only gives time and expertise to any project he undertakes, but that he gives of himself.

The tributes which continue to be paid to Nicky speak volumes for what has been the mainstay of his life. In 1991 he was the first member of the Maidenhead Rotarians to receive a Paul Harris Fellowship commendation – one of the organisation's top accolades. Nine years later he was honoured by Rotary International with the Service Above Self award in recognition of his outstanding efforts in fostering international goodwill and understanding. Nicky said then:

I was struck dumb by it – I never even knew it existed. I have never been lost for words, but I was at that time. It is such a prestigious award; I have been told that only 150 people worldwide a year get them. But I was terribly embarrassed.

Embarrassed or not, Nicky certainly lives up to Rotary's motto – Service Above Self.

* * *

In 1997 Matej Minac, a Slovak film director, was working on his film *All My Loved Ones* which tells the story of the gradual disintegration of a happy Jewish family in prewar Bohemia and the anguish they suffered because they refused to believe that the German occupation would lead to deportation and eventual death. Whilst Minac searched for some authentic means by which at least the family's young son could be saved, he came across the Czech version of my autobiography and thus learnt of Nicky's transports. He telephoned and begged me to try to persuade Nicky to permit his name and his story to be used in the film. 'It would make such an impact on the audience', he pleaded.

'Surely the story is strong enough to stand on its own', Nicky reasoned. 'Why use it in a fictional film?' But eventually he consented. I passed the message on and was promptly asked to fly to Prague for a meeting with Minac. He was already informed of my involvement in Nicky's life and matters relating to the rescue operation and that, together with Muriel Emanuel, I was writing a book on the subject.

Matej was intrigued, impressed and moved by what I told him; by the time I left Prague, he was determined to turn Nicky's impulsive comment into reality. I gladly agreed to help voluntarily with the project Minac had in mind – to make a documentary on Nicky and the children. I feel strongly that Nicky's role should be publicised wherever possible as an example and inspiration for now and the future. There are constantly so many others in desperate situations needing help.

The shooting of the documentary began in Prague the following March and took place mainly in the Hotel Evropa, where we were staying and where the whole story began. Attention of the media brought Nicky once again to the public eye; he soon became a household name and was treated as a hero. Despite his modest nature, both Grete and I noted that during this visit he was rather enjoying all the acclaim.

The highlight of the week was a grand reception in Nicky's honour given by the British Embassy, but the most meaningful event was the talk he gave and the discussion which followed at the Jewish Museum. The high esteem in which he is held by the general public was certainly evident that night. The hall was packed to bursting point, there was no standing room left; rather than go home disappointed, people squeezed into the adjacent passageway, so that they might hear what he had to say. I was proud to participate and was amazed how Nicky rose to the occasion at the end of a long, arduous day, part of which he spent on the bitterly cold, draughty railway station platform from which our train had departed all those years ago.

There was little time for relaxation and the Wintons looked back, almost longingly, to their previous trip to the Czech Republic when, in June 1995, they had joined our third school reunion, which was held, for a change, in the beautiful mediaeval town of Cesky Krumlov in southern Bohemia. Ruth Halova (Adler), the reunion's main organiser, initiated the twinning of her home town with Llanwrtyd Wells; exchanges also take place between local schools. Thus, the strong link between the Welsh and Czech communities continues through the second, and now third, generations.

At that time, I was also receiving a fair amount of publicity and recognition. The Czech edition of my book generated wide interest and was serialised unabridged on Prague Radio; Czech Television made a documentary film on my life, in which Nicky appeared. Both programmes were chosen to commemorate the fiftieth anniversary of Victory in Europe.

The four days spent in southern Bohemia, coupled with a short private stay in Prague, had been an idyllic holiday for the Wintons, with time to socialise with their extended family and to relax. In 1998 such opportunities were not to be found. Nicky stood up to the pressure and the intensive schedule magnificently and gave way to his exhaustion only when our plane left Prague; he slept all the way to London.

At Heathrow, only a taxi-driver greeted him – no dignitaries, no flowers, no official cars. 'Thank goodness they don't make such a fuss here in England', Nicky said, with some relief. 'I couldn't take any more. I need a holiday to get over the past week.' He got his holiday, a few weeks later, but it turned out rather differently than expected.

Whilst touring France with friends, Grete collapsed and was rushed to hospital. Nicky was devastated to learn that she had cancer. Grete was not just his wife and companion, she was his soulmate, his best friend, whose devotion and understanding had sustained him throughout their long marriage. He could not envisage a future without her. They both knew there was no hope, that it was only a matter of time. It was a shattering blow to all the family and everyone who knew and loved her.

After several weeks in hospital, Grete came home, physically

184

a shadow of her former self, but with her spirit as strong as ever. Friends and relatives rallied round, but it was Nicky's loving care and the strength of their relationship which fuelled Grete's willpower and determination to fight the disease as best she could. Nicky, now 89, adapted, took over most of Grete's former duties and put a temporary stop to most of his usual activities. They were anxious to spend together every moment they had left. In spite of the circumstances, both Nicky and Grete faced the outside world with courage, dignity, outward cheerfulness and ability to show interest in and concern for others.

This prompted Nicky to make an exception in the middle of June and attend briefly a 'Thank You Britain' reception at the Czech Embassy, for the pupils of our wartime school and for those who helped to save us. It was not easy for him to face so many old friends and to cope with the flood of genuine compassion everybody felt for him.

As it happened, the Czech ambassador, Dr Pavel Seifter, who has become a friend of Nicky's, had arrived in Britain in April 1939 as a babe in arms; he was just old enough to attend the Czech junior school in Shropshire for the last year of the war. He celebrated with us and joined us in Wales during the ensuing reunion.

The late Bill Barazetti, frail and supported by his two sons, but proud of his involvement in the rescue, was present. Charles Chadwick represented his late father, Trevor, appointed by Nicky as head of Prague's Children Section. My English mummy, then 101 years old, was one of the guests of honour. She sat in the front row between Nicky and the ambassador. She could barely hear a word of the speeches, but enjoyed every minute!

* * *

The Wintons had planned to hold a big party in the spring of 1999 to celebrate Nicky's ninetieth and Grete's eightieth birthdays, but the doctors advised them not to look that far ahead. As it happened, October 1998 marked their fiftieth wedding anniversary and, undeterred, they bravely decided to celebrate all three events then.

The 3rd of October was an unforgettable day, charged with emotions, tinged with sadness, yet filled with happiness, because Grete and Nicky were celebrating half a century of a wonderful partnership and were surrounded by family and close friends from different periods of their long lives. Yet it was impossible to brush the thought from my mind that many had come from near and far to bid Grete farewell.

Grete herself, so frail and thin, but with a smile that never left her face, spoke to everyone and ensured that the shadow of what was to come did not mar their big day. Nick and Barbara, their son and daughter, had organised the whole event; thoughtfully, they engaged a harpist to play Grete's favourite arias. The grandchildren – Laurence (ten) and Holly (seven), who waited on the guests – have brought much joy and laughter into their grandparents' lives.

The three generations of Nicky's 'other' family were represented by Anita Grosz, whose late father lived in the United States, by her baby daughter, Sophie, and myself. 'I suppose I am, respectively their adoptive father, grandfather and great-grandfather', Nicky announced to the gathering. 'That makes me very old.'

On the day of the party, the family reached an important decision. Nicky had been informed that, on 28 October, he was to be presented with the highest honour of the Czech Republic by President Vaclav Havel. Travelling abroad at such a time seemed unthinkable, but Grete was adamant that such an event was too important to miss. It was decided that their son, Nick, would accompany his father, whilst their daughter would stay with her mother.

At the grand ceremony in Hradcany Castle Nick was proud to witness his father receiving the Tomas Garrigue Masaryk Order from the president, in recognition of the saving of so many young lives. Nicky also had the honour of a private audience with the president.

Until their visit to Prague, Nick had not shown an interest in his father's rescue mission and usually shied away from the subject. During this short trip, he began to understand why his father was so highly thought of and to look at him with greater respect and pride. Their shared experience brought them very close.

* * *

In February 1999, at a special ceremony held for members of his family, Nicky was granted the Honorary Freedom of the Royal Borough of Windsor and Maidenhead for a lifetime dedicated to humanitarian activities. This award makes Nicky a member of a small elite group, which includes the Queen, the Queen Mother, the Duke of Edinburgh and Prince Charles.

Grete's cancer was not spreading as rapidly as predicted and she was at his side at the ceremony – Nicky's most treasured memory of that day. This was the last official function they were to share.

I valued the rare occasions when Grete felt up to joining Nicky for lunch in my cottage or when in the spring sunshine we were able to sit in their beautiful garden, sipping tea and munching the delicious cake regularly baked by a thoughtful friend. Watching Grete gradually fade away filled me with sadness and a sense of helplessness. They were coping so bravely – I was full of love and admiration for them both.

There were many areas in which I could help during these anxious times. I was handling many of Nicky's commitments. I was his spokeswoman, secretary, a buffer between him and the media, someone to whom anyone seeking information connected with the rescue mission could turn. Eventual interviews with Nicky for radio, television or for the press, usually took place in my cottage and resulted in floods of letters which needed my attention. The popularity of my book and the publicity it has enjoyed over the years gave me continuous opportunities to give talks to schools and adult groups on my life and Nicky's deed. His story goes hand in hand with mine and we both hope that by making the young people of today aware, through our personal experiences, what terrible consequences hate, violence and racism can have on mankind, they will view the atrocities, which continue to occur, in a different light and not turn away from human misery, but learn a lesson from our past for their future and strive to make the world a better place.

* * *

There was little time left for my private life and personal commitments; I tried my best not to neglect my partner and family where there were serious health problems, but during 1999 it was difficult, sometimes impossible to fit everything in. Writing this story was the first casualty and had to be put temporarily on a back burner.

Some projects could not be shelved; projects to which Nicky and I were already committed. Long before Grete fell ill, plans had been set in motion by the ROK to hold their second London Reunion of the Kindertransports in June 1999, to mark the sixtieth anniversary of our arrival in Britain. This presented an ideal opportunity to have our own meeting within the gathering. By then the number of children found had risen to more than 250 (sadly 48 are known to have died). This would give the newcomers the chance to meet their saviour.

The reunion was a memorable, highly emotional three-day event with more than 1,200 participants, amongst them 75 Winton children, some with their own children, even grandchildren, the youngest being Anita's baby, Sophie. There were distinguished speakers, lectures, workshops and discussion groups, culminating in a superb concert. This was to be the last reunion of its kind to take place.

On the first day, Nicky found himself on a panel of guest speakers, facing the whole assembly crammed into the huge auditorium. Totally unprepared, without notes and no time to think, he rose to the occasion with his usual wit and modesty: 'Good afternoon, Kinder, Kinder's Kinder and at least one Kinder's Kinder's Kinder, who I know is here,' he began, striking an instant rapport with the audience.

> As the original Kinder call me their adoptive father, it makes me feel much older than 90. I know my age, because when I stoop down to do up my shoelaces, I say to myself 'what else should I be doing whilst I am down here?'.

188

After recounting his story, disclaiming, as he always does, any great merit, he ended with the words:

I should like to issue a word of warning: we must remember, but just remembering is not enough. I don't think the world can go on living like that. I feel very strongly that people have to live more ethical, honest lives. We've got to take the reasons for remembering and the lessons we have learnt through remembering and see what good we can do, especially the people who have been saved.

Stephen Smith, founder/director of Beth Shalom Holocaust Memorial Centre, followed Nicky with a stirring speech and also warned us that we have to build a bridge from the past to the future – a bridge of Hope.

* * *

Grete passed away peacefully in her sleep on 28 August 1999. I had lost a caring friend – a woman of exceptional courage, dignity and extreme modesty. It was only at the Thanksgiving Service held in celebration of her life when I learnt that, during the war, as a young woman living alone in Copenhagen, she had harboured members of the Resistance and was eventually arrested and imprisoned by the Gestapo.

Nicky carries on, proudly, uncomplainingly. He masks his grief and the loneliness he feels, particularly in the home they had shared so happily for half a century; he is glad of his many friends and family and his continuing commitments.

An event which raised his spirits was the Prague premiere of Matej Minac's feature film *All My Loved Ones*, in October 1999, at which we were both honorary guests. Nicky's role, played by the British actor Rupert Graves, was comparatively small, but was so sensitively portrayed it brought the audience to their feet. Nicky was given a standing ovation. Near to tears he turned to me and said: 'If only Grete had lived to be here with me.' The presence of his daughter Barbara gave him comfort

189

and support and Barbara then became aware of the ongoing importance and meaning of her father's prewar deed and of the special bond between him and *his* children.

Again there were embassy receptions, television appearances, press conferences and joint talks. Many of the Winton children were with us, including Anita and Sophie. Joe Schlesinger flew in from Canada for the premiere and to continue interviewing Nicky. As one of Canada's most acclaimed television journalists who has a particularly close relationship with Nicky, Joe is the ideal person to take on a major role in the making of Minac's documentary on his life. The film is now completed and will be premiered in Prague and Bratislava in September 2001.

* * *

Over the years, Nicky attended many meetings and reunions; always anxious to please everyone, he visited many of the children. He even flew to Hungary to see two of them! He has also visited the United States several times, once as guest of honour at the Kindertransport Association Conference in Miami, where he was presented with a plaque expressing the gratitude and admiration of the Kinder of North America. (Anita told me that Nicky's speech was the most captivating event of the conference.) Most of all Nicky enjoyed staying with members of his extended family, with whom he forged many close, enduring friendships.

At the beginning of the new millennium Nicky went on a much needed holiday to Sarasota to the Groszs'. It was the second time he had visited the family. Unfortunately, he arrived seriously dehydrated and was so ill that the doctor recommended hospitalisation; this Nicky refused to accept. Anita's mother Kirsten, nursed him back to health and good humour, as noted by Hanus Grosz:

> We knew he must be feeling better when he showed us the silver medal (the MBE) which had been presented to him by the Queen, and told us, with a chuckle, 'I don't think

I've ever worn it. I pinned it to my pyjamas the day I got it so my wife would see it!'

Though still weak, Nicky stubbornly insisted on flying to Washington to revisit his good friends, the Masters and the Achters; he did not like the indirect flights and stopovers, but said the effort was worth it.

* * *

The second international academic conference 'Remembering for the Future 2000' took place in Oxford in July 2000, under the chairmanship of Dr Elisabeth Maxwell. A week of films, bringing a rememberance of the Holocaust and a message of peace and tolerance was screened concurrently at the ICA Cinema in London, culminating with the British premiere of *All My Loved Ones*. Nicky was surrounded by prominent guests, including Dr Maxwell – his friend and admirer, without whose efforts he may have remained unknown to this day. Also present were Dr Pavel Seifter ,the Czech ambassador, Karel Reisz and Matej Minac, the film directors, Lord Alf Dubs and Lady Grenfell-Baines.

On occasions such as these, Nicky stresses the same message – the message which was sent by him and read to the audience of *All My Loved Ones* at the film's US premiere at Palm Springs International Film Festival in January 2000:

It is right that these events should be remembered, but this rememberance must be used constructively – mankind must learn to be kind and tolerant and believe and live by the eternal values common to all religions. The fundamental effects of all religions must be taught and lead the way into the future.

* * *

For many years, in Nicholas' name and mine, I have tried to project this message through my talks, my autobiography and interviews. The publication of this book now presents another opportunity to reach out to a wider public, particularly to the young people of today, as I attempted to do on 27 January 2001 – Britain's first Holocaust Memorial Day. In a packed Westminster Central Hall, in the presence of His Royal Highness, the Prince of Wales, the Prime Minister, Tony Blair, and representatives from all walks of life and from all corners of the world, I had the honour to participate in this televised and much publicised unique event. I was able to pay tribute to Nicholas Winton and to all those to whom we, the former refugee children, owe our lives.

Vera Gissing's speech on Holocaust Memorial Day (Inaugural National Commemoration, Westminster Central Hall):

As one of the child refugees from Prague, I owe my life to Nicholas. But he could not have succeeded without the help of others.

When my foster-mother came to claim me, her first words were 'You shall be loved'. And those are the most important words any refugee child needs to hear.

Years later, I asked my foster-father why did he choose me. And he said, 'I knew I could not save the world, I knew I could not stop the war from starting, but I knew I could save ONE human soul. And as Chamberlain broke his pledge to Czechoslovakia, and as Jews were in the direst danger, I decided it must be a Czech-Jewish child.'

Tonight I would like to speak directly to children and young people – if YOU ever come to a time in your life when your help is needed, think of me and the 669 children who owe their lives to the moral courage of others.

At the time none of us realised how lucky we were, but now we know ...

Over 15,000 Czech Jewish children went through the camps; only a tiny fraction survived; so Nicky and his team saved the greater part of my generation. And not just us, but our children and grandchildren.

And he is with us tonight ...

27 January 2001